GOD SPEAKS:
Origins

GOD SPEAKS:
Origins

THIRD EDITION

Lynn L. Watkins, Th. D

Captured Splendor Books

For English editions of this work, all Scripture quotations are taken from *The American Standard Version* [ASV] of the Bible, unless otherwise noted. Scripture quotations marked [AMPC] are taken from *The Amplified Bible Classic*, copyright © 1954, 1958, 1962, 1964, 1965, 1987 by The Lockman Foundation. Those marked [AMP] are taken from the *Amplified Bible*, copyright © 2015 by the Lockman Foundation. Used by permission. Scripture quotations marked [WEB] are taken from the *World English Bible*, a Public Domain [no copyright] modern English translation of the Holy Bible. Scripture quotations marked [CJB] are taken from *The Complete Jewish Bible* by David H. Stern. Copyright © 1998. All rights reserved. Used by permission of Messianic Jewish Publishers, 6120 Day Long Lane, Clarksville, MD 21029. www.messianicjewish.net

For the Spanish edition of this book, all Bible quotations, unless otherwise noted, are from the *"Reina-Valera* 1960" (RVR1960).

While the author has made every effort to provide accurate Internet addresses at the time of publication, neither the publisher nor the author assumes any responsibility for errors or changes after publication.

For permission requests, write to the publisher, addressed "Attention: Permissions Coordinator," at the address below.

CITIOFBOOKS, INC.
3736 Eubank NE Suite A1
Albuquerque, NM 87111-3579
www.citiofbooks.com
Hotline: 1 (877) 389-2759
Fax: 1 (505) 930-7244

Ordering Information:

Quantity sales. Special discounts are available on quantity purchases by corporations, associations, and others. For details, contact the publisher at the address above.

Printed in the United States of America.

ISBN-13:   Paperback   979-8-89391-814-4
                eBook   979-8-89391-815-1

Library of Congress Control Number: 2025914716

To the members of the
Tuesday Night Bible Study, whose
questions sparked the birth of this
book, and my family and friends,
who have supported me throughout
my journey as an author.
And
to all who yearn to know the heart
of the Father.

Hear me, O Judah, and ye inhabitants of Jerusalem: believe in Jehovah your God, so shall ye be established; believe his prophets, so shall ye prosper.
[2 Chronicles 20:20]

He who has an ear, let him hear what the Spirit says to the assemblies.

[Revelation 2:7, WEB]

Contents

Preface to the Third Edition

When I completed the Second edition of *Divinely Commissioned: God's Delivery Service* in 2019, I closed my computer with a satisfied sigh, thinking, "Well, that's done. I wonder if I will ever write another book?"

I would surprise myself by writing several more books over the next few years. These books covered a variety of subjects, including the adventures of two donkeys, my testimony, a modern Christmas story, and one that focuses on the characteristics of the Bible. None of these concentrated on prophetic ministry.

A brief talk with a book publisher made me take another look at the second edition of my first book. I discovered that my book had become dated! During the time I was exploring other topics, public interest in the prophetic grew exponentially. Prophetic books and conferences multiplied. While many legitimate, mature prophets arose, the number of false prophets and false apostles also increased significantly. Today, hundreds of self-proclaimed prophets and apostles flood the internet with their videos and teachings, and not everyone can distinguish between the true and the false. This situation does not surprise me, for the enemy constantly tries to steal from God's people and pervert God's blessings.

Therefore, I sought to update and expand my book to make *Divinely Commissioned* more accessible and valuable to those studying the prophetic. However, I ran into a problem. The first edition of *Divinely Commissioned* was set with small type and ran almost 280 pages. The second edition was longer. The third edition, with its additional material, ran to more than 500 pages! In addition, the creation of a Spanish translation required me to expand certain portions to acknowledge Roman Catholic and Orthodox beliefs.

Therefore, I have decided to retitle the book and divide the work into a three-volume series.

- Volume 1 will focus on the origin and early development of prophets, prophecy, and prophetic ministry.
- Volume 2 will focus on Jesus, the Living Word of God, and how His life, death, and resurrection transformed prophetic ministry.
- Volume 3 explores prophetic ministry in the New Testament era.

As noted earlier, this book and its companion volumes greatly expand the information of earlier editions. I have included materials previously found only in the study guides. I have also expanded the bibliography. Another significant change has been my transition from footnotes to endnotes. This change enables purchasers of e-books to access the additional material found in those notes for the first time.

The book has also been reset with a new font, and quotations and endnotes are printed in a larger size for improved readability.

In this book, I have quoted from the *American Standard Bible, the Amplified Bible Classic, the Amplified Bible, the Complete the Complete Jewish Bible, and the World English Bible*. Like the *American Standard* translation of the Bible, the WEB is a public domain [no copyright] translation. I selectively used these translations when I thought the wording of a particular translation gave insight into what might be difficult passages to understand in the *American Standard* translation. I originally chose to include quotations from *The American Standard Version* for English-speaking people for three reasons:

- First, this is an "open source" Bible, meaning this translation has no copyright [as is the WEB].
- Second, the wording is just different enough from the King James Version [also an "open source" version of the Bible] that, I hope, you are forced to slow down and consider what you are reading when you come to each portion of Scripture.

The third reason is my personal attachment to this translation of God's Word. My father owned a 1945 imprint of *The American Standard* Bible printed by the University of Chicago Press; this edition was formatted like a novel. As a child, this Bible drew my attention and interest. That aged volume sits on the bookshelf behind my desk today.

What has not changed is my desire for readers to discover how much God loves them and wants to communicate with them. May this new edition provide readers with a basic understanding of prophetic ministry, for God wants to communicate with humanity and express His love for humanity. Prophetic ministry is one of the many ways He chooses to do so.

Lynn Watkins
October 2024

For my Spanish brethren, please note that for the Spanish this book, all Bible quotations, unless otherwise noted, are from the "Reina-Valera 1960" (RVR1960).

Preface to The Second Edition

I am grateful to each of you who shared your insightful evaluations of the original edition of this book. Your feedback has been the cornerstone of this second edition, making you an integral part of its evolution.

There were three main reasons for publishing this second edition of *Divinely Commissioned: God's Delivery Service* so quickly after the release of the first edition.

- Firstly, I wanted to provide a less academically oriented book. While I have provided more quotations from the Word of God in this edition, most academic quotations have been omitted. This change will allow the book to be translated and released overseas.
- Secondly, I also wanted to create an edition for release on electronic media.
- Finally, I tried to incorporate additional material and make corrections based on the gracious feedback I received.

With these goals in mind, this second edition contains:

- Typographical and punctuation corrections.
- A slightly larger font for greater ease in reading.
- The reworking of certain concepts.

I have included a selected bibliography of references at the end of this volume. The works listed have profoundly affected the development of this book and my understanding of prophetic ministry. These selected resources will help readers who want to learn more.

If English is not your primary language but you are reading this in English, I recommend you keep your personal Bible alongside this book [and an English language Bible, if you have one]. Having both Bibles will help you navigate this book's references, as chapter and verse numbering systems differ among various translations.

May the Lord encourage you to dig deeper and learn more about prophetic ministry. May this book be a stepping stone in your journey of learning and growth.

Lynn Watkins
January 21, 2019

Acknowledgments

"No one writes a book in a vacuum." I originally wrote those words over six years ago. The statement was true then; it is true now. First and foremost, I thank Jesus Christ for sending our Guide and Paraclete, the Holy Spirit. I could achieve nothing without the Holy Spirit. I am also thankful for the Christian scholars and believers whose research and teachings blessed my Biblical studies. I am also grateful to those who have mentored and disciplined me. I extend special thanks to Pastor Jerry Clevenger, Dr. Max Flynn, Dr. Bill Hamon, Bishop Houston Miles, Mrs. Evelyn Miles, Dr. Randall Langley, Prophet Jakob Durokovic, Pastor Kay Durokovic, and Pastors Howard and Rosella Ridings. These people all spoke into my life at critical points:

- Pastor Clevenger continually blessed me through sharing his life and wisdom with my husband, Mike, and me.
- Dr. Max Flynn taught me about the gifts of the Spirit [and the importance of digging into the Scriptures to benefit myself and others].
- Dr. Hamon provided most of my prophetic training through conferences, seminars, and the Christian International School of Theology. He is my father [along with Dr. Max Flynn] in the prophetic and my ministerial covering as head of Christian International.
- Bishop Houston and Evelyn Miles, humble visionaries in the kingdom, taught me and released me into

ministry through Evangel Fellowship conferences overseas.

- Dr. Langley served as my pastor, supervised much of my advanced theological education, and presented me with my Th.D. from the Christian Life School of Theology.
- Howard and Rosella Ridings loved and mentored me. Pastor Howard encouraged me to finish my theological studies and obtain my ministerial license. They believed in me when others did not.
- And I wish to thank Prophetess and Pastor Kay Durakovic; she and her husband Jakob, have openly shared the blessings and challenges of living and walking as Jesus' prophets today.

Since the first edition of this work was published, Jakob Durakovic, Howard Ridings, Max Flynn, and Jerry Clevenger have entered the Lord's presence. They served the Lord faithfully and great is their reward. I bless their memory.

I am grateful to Mrs. Frances Seel for her tireless work in editing the various editions of this book. It was sometimes painful to receive her corrections, but the book truly needed her input. If any punctuation, grammatical, or layout errors remain, it is not because of Mrs. Seel. She has worked tirelessly to overcome my faults.

I also thank Monica and Bruce Valentien for their suggestions and input. They not only reviewed this third edition with fresh eyes, but Monica also caught formatting errors in the manuscript.

How can I express my thanks to my family? They patiently endured all the time I have spent studying and writing. They have put up with various irritations, such as "I just need to finish this page!" [a five-minute delay that sometimes took an hour], "Have you seen the book I was reading?" or multiple late dinners. My husband, Michael, has been kind and patient throughout the time taken for the writing, editing, publication process. He has now had to endure this entire process multiple times!

Finally, I want to give God our Father all the glory and honor. There would be nothing to write about except His stupendous, overwhelming love for us. How amazing is our Father, Who made people, knowing that people would disobey Him! What can I say about the love of Jesus, Who died for us so we could again be in a relationship with the Father? My choice to capitalize the pronouns and nouns relating to the Godhead is just a small token of respect for the Creator of all. He is the source of any good found in this book.

Lynn L Watkins

July 24, 2024

P.S.—I pray Holy Spirit will speak His truth into your heart through this book and give you a greater revelation of God's love for you.

GOD SPEAKS:
ORIGINS

GOD'S REVELATION IN THE OLD TESTAMENT

For if the mystery concealed of old is made manifest to the Apostles through the prophetic writings, and if the prophets, being wise men, understood what proceeded from their own mouths, then the prophets knew what was made manifest to the Apostles.
- Origen

CHAPTER I

INTRODUCTION

Welcome! If you have opened this book, I assume you are interested in learning more about Biblical prophecy and how it could affect your life. You are not alone; the history of humanity records man's search:

- For an ultimate, divine being [that is, God],
- For a relationship with that Divine being that resulted in a satisfying life for the individual,
- And to discover the reason and purpose for the Divine being's creation of men and women.

Different philosophies claim to know the answers to those questions. However, the Bible, the ancient book belonging to both the Jewish people and the Christian Church, declares that it alone contains the answers that God, known as the "Elohim," "Yahweh," "Yeshua," "the Alpha, and Omega", gave to man's questions.

In reality, the "Bible" is not a single book; it is a collection of books. Sixty-six books comprise the Bible.[1] These sixty-six books are divided into "The Old and New Testaments." [The Jewish people restrict their Bible to what Christians call "The Old Testament"; these books focus on the covenant God gave to Moses for the Hebrews.] Nevertheless, theologically and thematically, the Bible is one book that reveals God's love for humanity and His desire for fellowship with us.

One of the most unique features of the Bible is the account of the various prophecies recorded within it. "Prophecy" is another name for one of the ways that God communicates with people. Please note that I said, "God[2] communicates..." for God is the One reaching out to people. The Bible contains accounts of God speaking to people through dreams, visions, angels, and individuals called "prophets."

This volume provides an overview of the origin and purpose of prophecy and prophetic ministry.[3] However, the idea and study of prophecy is controversial, filling people with questions.

- Did or does God really speak to people? Or are Biblical prophecies just a primitive people's attempts to explain events?
- Are all prophecies warnings and condemnations?
- How do we know God is speaking through someone?
- Why should we care if God spoke to people in the past?
- Does God still speak to people today?

Some of the Church's teachings complicate rather than clarify the answers to these fundamental questions.

Many believers have been taught that prophetic ministry disappeared after the Bible was canonized[4] [that is, after church officials decided which books to include in the Bible]. Others have been taught that prophecy is irrelevant, as focusing on a study of prophecy distracts the believer from doing the Lord's work and leads to neglect of evangelical outreach.

I cannot agree with these perspectives. I base my opinion on my studies of the Word of God. However, my quest to study and understand prophetic ministry grew out of my unique encounters with God when I first became a disciple of Jesus.

Before I accepted Jesus Christ as my Lord and Savior, I had heard about God in the mainline Protestant church my parents took me to until I was about twelve years old. As I listened to the stories of God, I thought, if God exists, then why doesn't He perform the signs, wonders, and miracles that He did in the Bible? Why doesn't He still speak to us directly or through angels or His prophets? Why is attending church boring when the Bible contains action-packed, exciting stories?

However, when I was eighteen, I discovered the Truth: God speaks and moves today! God is real! He still does miracles and wonders! I had based my belief that God did not exist [or did not exist as described in the Bible] on misinformation, ignorance, and my own hard heart. I learned, however, that there have been times when the Church [that is the united, universal Body of Believers past and present] had ignored or received few manifestations of God's supernatural presence. Yet God had not "gone away." Among those who believed in God and His Word, He has always shown Himself mighty. God is the same great "I AM" that was, is, and is to come!

Nonetheless, as a newborn believer, I did not know how God moved and interacted with His people. I was a "spiritual baby, understanding nothing" [anonymous]. I needed the pure spiritual milk of God's word [1 Peter 2:2].

Pearls before swine

In those early days, as a believer who only had a smattering of Biblical knowledge, I thought that the gifts and ministries of God—including prophecy—were the "pearls" of God [see Matthew 7:6] that were not to be wasted on the unsaved "swine" [people like the unsaved me]. I assumed all true Christians fully embraced the nine gifts of the Holy Spirit [as explained in 1 Corinthians 12:7-11] in their personal and church lives. I thought believers used ESP[5] [or detected some spiritual aura] to discern between "real" Christians and the

"fake" Christians. I also thought the gifts and ministries were practiced in the Church only when the "true believers" were separated from the "fake" believers. My ideas were wrong!

Even though I was woefully ignorant of God's word, when I read 1 Corinthians 12 and 1 Corinthians 14 [see vs. 3-5] for the first time, I enthusiastically said, "Yes, Lord! Make ME a prophet!" Now, God knew what I was thinking: I wanted to see God move in power and to know Him better, but I also thought being a prophet would be fun. [My idea of prophets had come from watching old movies.] Being a prophet would make me famous and garner me a lot of positive attention. [I had no idea of the problems that prophets faced.]

I look back at that eager young [but self-centered] girl and laugh. God must have laughed, too. However, God saw past all my selfish desires to my heart's core, where I truly desired to please and honor my heavenly Father. He answered, "Yes, I will make you My prophet—but it will take time, little one." By God's grace, I have matured, becoming conformed to the image of Jesus.[6] I have come to realize:

- The gifts and callings of God are not toys to entertain but tools to set the captive free.
- The most important aspect of a relationship with God is not your gift or ministry but the love relationship you develop with the Lord.
- You can do nothing without God, but if you yield your life to Him, Jesus will lead you on a great adventure.
- I have also realized that in many churches, that is, the various parts of the Body of Christ, there is a great fear of the prophetic gifts being released within the Body.
- We cannot be who God calls us to be, unless we become saturated in God's Word.

This fear of the prophetic has grown out of a misunderstanding and misuse of the prophetic gifts within the Church by gifted

but immature people, and assaults launched by spiritual enemies. Nevertheless, these misunderstandings and fears can be overcome or broken through the power of the Spirit. God does not want you or anyone else to live in fear.

Why study prophecy

Yet, you may wonder if you really need to make a "big deal" out of studying prophetic ministry? After all, there are only so many hours in the day and so much time left in this old world. Believers are called to conform to Christ's image [Galatians 4:19, 1 Corinthians 11:1] and to keep their focus on Jesus, so why is the study of Bible prophecy vital for Christians today?

- What specific blessings come from the study of prophecy today?
- What can make dealing with all the questions, misunderstandings, and fears surrounding prophecy worthwhile?
- <u>How can a ancient gift from God transform my daily life?</u>

<u>The main reason to study prophecy is that prophecy is a tool used by God to bring you into a more intimate relationship with Him.</u> Take a moment and reread this sentence. Savor this truth: God wants to have intimacy with you! Now, you may need a paradigm shift —a complete change in your thinking —to grasp that God wants to have close, personal fellowship with you. Take a moment and think about this:

<u>God wants to spend time with you, to have you share your heart with Him, and to allow Him to share His heart with you.</u> Remember this: Prophecy's fullest dimensions reveal the very heart, the very thoughts of God. [Consider what this means!]

Another way to express this is to call prophecy a love letter from God. Every prophecy expresses God's love and concern

for humanity. Prophets are God's divinely appointed messengers, commissioned by our Father to carry His love letters to His people. Think of that for a moment! God wants you to have uniquely personal fellowship with Him and the pleasure of knowing His perfect love.

God also wants you to experience the joy of sharing that love with others. He wants you to receive His love and show His love to a world that does not show what love is. However, to present God's nature and heart to a dying world, our faith must flow out of our relationship with the Lord. God wants you to take up His divine commission to share His love with others, but only after personally experiencing His love.

Prophecy is intimately involved in the maturation of your faith. A proper, well-balanced understanding of prophecy does not distract any believer from living a fruitful life of service to the Lord. Instead, it should help you, for prophecy can bring you into a closer relationship with the Lord! Prophecy can reveal God's will and purpose for your life. In the Old Testament, God revealed His will and plans to His people through the words of the prophets. The New Testament declares that a study of prophecy should keep you on course in your Christian walk, enabling you to grow closer to Christ. The Apostle Peter wrote:

> *⁷But the end of all things is at hand: be ye therefore of sound mind, and be sober unto prayer: ⁸<u>above all things being fervent in your love among yourselves</u>; . . .⁹using hospitality one to another without murmuring: ¹⁰<u>according as each hath received a gift, ministering it among yourselves, as good stewards of the manifold grace of God; if any man speaketh, speaking as it were oracles of God</u>; if any man ministereth, ministering as of the strength which God supplieth: <u>that in all things God may be glorified through Jesus Christ, whose is the glory and the</u>*

dominion for ever and ever. Amen [1 Peter 4:7-11.
Emphasis mine].

One of the ways you minister in love is by speaking and receiving the words and warnings of God [that's prophetic ministry]. You glorify God when you minister as Jesus' servant in all areas of gifting, including the prophetic realm. The Bible reveals that God will "chasten" [or discipline] you because He loves you and wants you to walk rightly and in blessing; prophecy, as recorded in Scripture, was one of God's direct methods for God to reveal His will and His correction to people.

As part of *"the good fight of faith"* [see 1 Timothy 6:12], you must use prophecy appropriately [by applying prophetic principles correctly] when praying or engaging in spiritual warfare. Prophecy is vital in spiritual warfare, for prophecy can reveal the enemy's tactics and provide spiritual direction for your prayers.

Paul also wrote in 1 Timothy 6:11-14 that you are to fight the good fight of faith and that you are to keep *"the whole body of principles blameless, above reproach, until the appearing of our Lord Jesus Messiah"* [v. 14]. You cannot obey Paul's command and ignore prophecy and the prophetic gifts, for Revelation 19:10 tells us that *"the testimony of Jesus is the spirit of prophecy"* [emphasis mine].

1 Thessalonians 5:20 specifically warns you not to despise or dishonor prophesying. 1 Thessalonians 5:23 indicates that the proper understanding and acceptance of Biblical prophecy seems to be involved in a believer's Biblical sanctification. These Biblical warnings should always be taken seriously.

> *15See that no one returns evil for evil to anyone, but always follow after that which is good... 16Always rejoice. 17Pray without ceasing. 18In everything give*

thanks, for this is the will of God in Christ Jesus toward you. [19]Don't quench the Spirit. [20]Don't despise prophecies. [21]Test all things, and hold firmly that which is good. [22]Abstain from every form of evil. [23]May the God of peace himself sanctify you completely. May your whole spirit, soul, and body be preserved blameless at the coming of our Lord Jesus Christ.1 Thessalonians 5:15-23, WEB, emphasis mine].

Some other reasons to study prophecy:

- Quantity — Almost one-third of the Bible is specifically prophetic. If you ignore prophecy, you are ignoring one-third of the Bible!
- Identification — Prophecy identified and verified that Jesus was the Messiah when He first came. The information revealed in the various, written prophecies about His second coming can protect believers from the lies and deceptions of false messiahs and the anti-Christ [2 John 1:7; 2 Thessalonians 2:2-12; Matthew 24:5, 24; Mark 13:6].
- Revelation — Prophecy reveals God's love for man despite man's failings, the fate of Satan, and the triumph of God and His people. Prophecies for people today offer encouragement, direction, and insight into God's plans for their individual lives. Paul stated that God reveals what you could never imagine through His Spirit [1 Corinthians 2:9-10]. Prophecy can warn you about potential mistakes and strengthen you during trials or tests.
- Educational — The revelations revealed in prophecy can be very enlightening or educational. Prophecy can underline moral teachings and promote spiritual growth. Prophecy can help you understand God's perspective on current events in your local church, town, country, and the world. Prophecy can also signify the "season" you, your church, or your nation may be

experiencing. As stated, Biblical prophecy [especially prophetic words included in the Bible] warns you of events occurring before Jesus returns.

- Weapon of Warfare—God has given us the prophetic word to be a weapon for spiritual warfare [Exodus 10:21-13:36; Joshua 6:13-27. See also 2 Corinthians 10:3-5; Ephesians 6:12].
- Cyclical—Prophecy generally seems to run in cycles [it repeats itself], and a single prophecy can have more than one fulfillment. A well-known example of "cyclical prophecy" is found in Isaiah:

⁷Therefore the Lord himself will give you a sign: behold, a virgin shall conceive, and bear a son, and shall call his name Emmanuel [Isaiah 7:14].

Anyone who has heard Handel's Messiah is familiar with this verse. Matthew 1:18-23 refers to this verse as a testimony that Jesus was the Messiah. However, when you review Isaiah chapter 7 and examine this verse, you will see that the original prophecy about a virgin birth was spoken to King Ahaz. God was telling King Ahaz not to worry about the kingdom of Aram; God would help. Prophecies may have multiple meanings, even if the one receiving the prophecy initially does not realize this truth.

There <u>are</u> serious concerns about prophetic ministry of all types. Some of these objections have deep historical roots in the teaching of various denominations, and some have arisen recently due to prophetic misuses. Some concerns are less defined but flow from uneasiness over the idea that prophecy even exists at all!

The idea that God talks to and through people may make you uncomfortable. Still, you must understand that prophecy is part of your inheritance and your responsibility as a Christian. A mature understanding of prophecy is part of growing up and maturing in Christ [Hebrews 6:1-3]. Attempting to

grow spiritually while ignoring prophecy leads to stilted or unbalanced growth and a flawed understanding of God.

Always remember that the prophetic words of both the Old Testament and the New Testament serve as encouragement to remain faithful to God and to grow strong in your faith. Jesus gave you the Holy Spirit to be your Guide and Counselor [John 14:16-17, 26:15-26]. When the Holy Spirit came, He came bearing gifts for you, including the gift of prophecy.

> *Now concerning spiritual things, brothers, I don't want you to be ignorant.... ³Therefore I make known to you that no man speaking by God's Spirit says, "Jesus is accursed." No one can say, "Jesus is Lord," but by the Holy Spirit.*
>
> *⁴Now there are various kinds of gifts, but the same Spirit. ⁵There are various kinds of service, and the same Lord. ⁶There are various kinds of workings, but the same God, who works all things in all. ⁷But to each one is given the manifestation of the Spirit for the profit of all. ⁸For to one is given through the Spirit the word of wisdom, and to another the word of knowledge, according to the same Spirit; ⁹to another faith, by the same Spirit; and to another gifts of healings, by the same Spirit; ¹⁰and to another workings of miracles; and to another prophecy; and to another discerning of spirits; to another different kinds of languages; and to another the interpretation of languages. ¹¹But the one and the same Spirit produces all of these, distributing to each one separately as he desires [1 Corinthians 12:1, 3-11. WEB].*

You need to remember that Jesus has granted prophetic ministry to the Church to be a blessing [1 Corinthians 14:26-40]. Jesus established the Office of the Prophet for the maturation of the Church [Ephesians 4:11-16]. If we avoid

prophecy and prophetic ministry, we may fail to provide the edification, exhortation, or comfort that another brother or sister in Christ may need [1 Corinthians 14:3]. If we shun prophecy, we handicap ourselves and may never fulfill the ministry to which we are called, whether within or outside the Church. If we neglect prophetic giftings, we may never enter the office that God may have chosen for us [especially that of the Office of the Prophet or an Apostle] for failing to believe and obey Him in all things. To receive God's blessings and be His conduit to the Church and the world, we must know what prophecy is—and what it is not.

We also need to remember that we are told explicitly in 1 Thessalonians 5:19-22 to do three things:

- To prove all things [including prophetic words]. Proving prophecy involves evaluating and testing the quality, worth, genuineness, and truth of the prophetic word.
- To hold fast [to hold on tightly] to what is good *["what is good and acceptable and the will of God,"--See Romans 12:2]*. We must hold fast to prophetic words.
- To *"despise not prophecy" or "Don't despise prophecies," [1 Thessalonians 5:20, WEB]*. In other words, to pay attention, listen to, and appreciate valid prophetic words that have been proven.

God knew that certain individuals would attempt to deceive others and claim to have prophetic words. Nevertheless, we must not reject prophecy and God's blessings because of the fakes and frauds. We must remember:

> *Surely the Lord GOD does nothing Without revealing His secret plan [of the judgment to come] To His servants the prophets. The lion has roared! Who will not fear? The Lord GOD has spoken [to the prophets]. Who can but prophesy? [Amos 3:7-*

8, AMPC. See also Genesis 18:17, Jeremiah 23:22, Revelation 10:7]

We must listen when God chooses to speak, for He always speaks for our benefit. You and I must not let discomfort or laziness stop us from receiving the blessings or the protection from danger God wants to give us.

Remember what Amos wrote: God will do nothing until He has shown His plans to His prophets [Amos 3:7]. God will reveal His blessings through His prophets and warn us of danger and judgments. It would be foolish not to listen to what God is saying either through His written word [the Bible] or His spoken words [prophetic ministry]. It's "beyond foolish" to hear His words but ignore them! There are many misunderstandings about prophetic ministry, but the misunderstandings and fears that surround all types of prophetic ministry in and outside the Church can only be overcome or broken by:

- <u>Studying</u> Biblical prophecy [if we do not carefully study a subject, we cannot form an informed or wise conception of that subject]. God wants us to grow in our understanding and wisdom.
- <u>Understanding</u> God's purposes in releasing the prophetic gifts. We must never forget that God only gives good gifts to His children.
- <u>And trusting</u> God to show us how to use and evaluate these gifts properly. This includes learning to discern between the gift of prophecy, the ministry of prophecy, and or the work of an Office Prophet.

If you study Biblical prophecy to understand God's purposes in releasing the prophetic gifts and trust God to show you how to use these gifts properly, you will be blessed. You can discover a deeper connection with God that has been hindered by fear, ignorance, and incorrect teaching. Fear and mistrust

are from the enemy, but the Lord never wants fear to control us. You and I have much to learn about prophetic ministry, but we have a Father Who is eager to teach us!

Why This Book

Many courses discuss prophecy, and many books have been written about prophecy. However, few books address the origins of prophecy and how prophetic ministry developed and changed during the Old Testament era.

This book is particularly designed to help believers discern the truth about God's gift of prophecy and prophetic ministry by introducing the reader to the origins of prophetic ministry. While this survey work cannot provide a comprehensive study of every prophet in the Old Testament or every biblical prophecy in detail, this book can lay a foundational understanding. Through this study, the reader will gain an overview of the development of Biblical prophecy in Old Testament times[6] and a basic understanding foundational for further prophetic studies.

Specifically, through this historical study of prophets and prophetic ministry, from the time of Creation until the end of the Old Testament era, I hope:

- To dispel fear and create a basic biblical understanding of prophetic ministry.
- To answer the questions that believers have about the prophetic.
- To remind believers that God will show them what is proper and acceptable in His sight.
- Grasp the importance of prophetic ministry among God's people.

This volume can be your first step in your study of prophecy and prophetic ministry. My purpose for this book [and this

entire series] succeeds <u>if you, the student, understand how much the Father loves you and desires to fellowship with and communicate to you and others.</u>

God has always desired to talk and fellowship with His creation. The Fall of humanity in the Garden did not destroy this desire. God gave prophetic ministry to promote knowledge of and intimacy with the Father and to bridge the separation between God and humankind that resulted from the Fall. Through this study, I pray that every believer enters the fellowship and intimacy God desires to have with us.

So, let us reject fear and discover God's perspective toward the prophetic. Let's begin by approaching God's throne of grace boldly [see Hebrews 4:16] and ask God to help us discover His purposes for prophetic ministry throughout the ages and in our lives today.

Dear Father,

Thank you, Lord, for creating humanity and wanting to fellowship with us. Thank you, for choosing to speak to us through prophecy. Thank you, Father, for those men and women, living both now and in the past, who took up Your divine commission and entered Your service as Your prophets. Give us ears, O Lord, to hear and correctly evaluate what the prophets are speaking.

Lord, help us understand Your purposes for prophecy and allow Your Holy Spirit to train us to experience prophecy correctly. Teach us to discern what biblical prophecy is and is not. Please give us the courage to listen to what You want to teach and empower us to walk in that teaching. Make Your will and purpose clear to all who read this work. We pray, Father, that through this book, You are glorified and Your wisdom and greatness are declared. Protect us from vain imaginings or thinking more highly of

ourselves than we ought to. Father God, We want to know Your truth in all things. Teach us about the prophetic, O Lord. Open our eyes to Your Word and give us revelation. Grant that everyone who reads this book draws closer to You. May everything we learn excite us about Who You are and enable us to glorify Your Name. We ask this in Jesus' name. Amen.

Endnotes for Chapter I: Introduction

[1] The Protestant canon has 66 books. The Roman Catholic canon has 73 books. The Orthodox canon varies between 75-81 books depending on the tradition of the various Orthodox churches.

[2] God—the English term for the Alpha-Omega, the Great Creator, sometimes referred to as "Elohim" or "Yahweh" in Hebrew.

[3] Prophetic ministry is simply the work of a prophet.

[4] The rabbis generally teach that prophecy ended with the close of the Old Testament canon. Of course, most Jews do not accept the New Testament as canon. However, many Christian denominations still reject modern prophetic ministry.

[5] This is NOT an endorsement for ESP [Extra Sensory Perception] or any other ungodly method of obtaining knowledge. I chose long ago to put aside the unrighteous thing [Ephesians 4:22; Colossians 3:8].

[6] Like the song says, "He's still working on me; to make me what I ought to be…" [He's Still Working on Me", Joel Hemphill, *The Best of the Hemphills*, 2007]. Or as Paul wrote,

> *Not that I have already obtained, or am already made perfect, but I press on, that I may take hold of that for which also I was taken hold of by Christ Jesus [Philippians 3:12, WEB].*

CHAPTER II

DEFINITIONS: A PLETHORA OF "P'S"

Review

In the last chapter, we established that believers should understand all aspects of prophecy and prophetic ministry. While the idea of God speaking to and through people today may make many people uncomfortable, God uses prophecy to help His church mature, grow in unity, and become more like Jesus. Any attempt to grow spiritually while ignoring prophecy leads to stilted or unbalanced growth and a flawed understanding of God. To continue our conversation and develop the insight and wisdom we seek, believers must have a shared understanding of the definitions for the terms we use.

Therefore, having decided to study prophecy and the prophetic, you now face your first challenge: define the word "prophecy" and other terms used in discussing prophetic ministry. To communicate correctly, you and I must agree on the actual meaning of the words we use.

This problem is complicated by some people's tendency to confuse biblical prophecy with ungodly fortune-telling or divination. The tendency to call any inspirational or insightful leader a "prophet" is also confusing. These people's definitions and understanding of "prophet" and "prophecy"

are inconsistent with how the Bible defines these terms. So, in this chapter, I will explain the following terms—

- Prophecy
- Prophesy
- Prophet
- Prophetic Song [The Song of the Lord]
- Prophetic Acts
- Prophetic Presbytery

—according to Biblical truth. I shall do so to the best of my ability by the Lord's will and power!

Prophecy

How should we define "prophecy"? What does the word "prophecy" mean? In its purest sense, a "prophecy" is a message from God given to a person to deliver or to share with someone else. A more formal definition of the word states that prophecy is a communication inspired by the Divine that reveals the Divine will and purpose.

This message from the Divine may take many forms. Prophecies may consist of written or spoken words, but prophecy may also consist of a dream [while a person sleeps], a "waking" vision, or a type of physical manifestation. Sometimes, only the prophet hears or sees the vision; at other times, other people can be involved [See 2 Kings 6:15-17]. Thus, the message from God may be seen or heard and may include symbols or poetry.

In the Old Testament, a prophecy may also be referred to as "an oracle" [Numbers 24:2, 15; Isaiah 13:1; Malachi 1:]¹, "a burden" [Nahum 1:1; Habakkuk 1:1], or "the Word of the Lord" [Genesis 15:1, 4; 1 Samuel 3:1]. Both the Old Testament and the New Testament record instances of prophets physically acting out a prophecy for their audience:

- Isaiah [Isaiah 20—went naked for three years]
- Jeremiah [Jeremiah 32—bought land]
- Ezekiel [Ezekiel 12:1-8—demonstrated that the people faced exile by his actions of carrying his belongings away.]
- And Agabus [Acts 21:10-11—acted out Paul's arrest]

What makes all these messages unique <u>is not that the messages were "true" but that God sent them.</u>

Let me explain what this means. Remember that I began by saying that prophecy was and is a <u>message from Yahweh</u> God, the Elohim, and Creator. I can write you a letter, call you on the phone, or act out my message; but I am giving you a prophecy only if that message is from God, and not from any other source. Now, I could tell you that I have carefully studied the sky and know you'd better carry an umbrella today, for it will rain. My statement, however, even if it comes true, is not a prophecy; it is merely a prediction based on studying weather conditions.

<u>True prophecy always contains a message that originates in the Godhead.</u> Simply put, prophecy is always a message from God. If a message is not from God, it is not a true prophecy. It does not matter if the message seems valid, causes your toes to tingle, or even if thunder, lightning, or a miraculous event accompanies the message.

God might choose a friend, a pastor, or even a donkey [Numbers 22:20-33] to convey His message, but <u>true prophecy is always a message from God Himself.</u> The friend, the pastor, or the donkey is merely a messenger who carries out his divine commission to deliver the message that God has given. That may seem obvious, but I want you to dwell on that truth until it is part of your soul. <u>True prophecy is a message or communication from God delivered through one of God's servants.</u> Simply put, prophecy is a message from God, and

18

the one delivering God's message is God's personal "delivery" person, a member of God's "divine delivery service."

Nevertheless, it is also a testimony of the grace and glory of God that He usually trusts individual human beings to relay His message to humanity. When God moves upon someone to deliver a prophetic message, His messenger does not become a "zombie"[2] or lose his individual personality. While people may be temporarily overwhelmed by the love and presence of God, they remain themselves, with their own quirks, abilities, vocabulary, and understandings. Thus, each messenger [the prophet or prophetess] relays the words of God in his or her distinct style. This truth is the meaning of the Greek term *"theopuesta"* [this Greek word is translated as "God is speaking," "God-breathed," or "God is speaking His word through people"]. Peter explains the wonder of *"theopuesta"* this way,

> For no prophecy ever came by the will of man: but men spake from God, being moved by the Holy Spirit [1 Peter 1:21].

Now, when I speak of "true prophets" and "true prophecy," I also acknowledge that there are false prophecies and false prophets. Remember that the Bible says Satan often disguises himself as an angel of light [2 Corinthians 11:14]. He has, does, and will attempt to distract and mislead people by counterfeiting prophecy. We will discuss true and false prophecies in more detail later. The point is to understand that authentic Biblical prophecy is a message from God [and only the God of the Bible] and that God uses individuals to deliver His message to others.

We can divide prophecy [the message God gives man] into two general types [The Old and New Testaments contain each type]. The kind of prophecy most people are familiar with is "foretelling" or predictive prophecy. Foretelling prophecies

refer to events that may occur in the future; these are forecasts of coming events. All the prophecies of the Old Testament that speak of the coming birth of the Messiah are predictive or foretelling prophecies. The prophecies that predict the destruction of evil cities [such as Nineveh in the book of Nahum] and the judgment of nations are also foretelling prophecies.

However, while predictive prophecies tend to stick in our imagination, they may not be as important as the second type of prophecy, God's "forthtelling" or declarative messages. Forthtelling prophecies reveal God's perspective on a present situation. They reveal God's heart to us.

Let me illustrate what I mean by providing some biblical examples of both types of prophecies.

Predictive prophecies: foretelling

Let's look at 1 Samuel 10:2-7. In this passage, Samuel anoints Saul king over Israel and tells Saul five specific things that will shortly occur.

> *²When thou art departed from me today, then thou shalt find two men by Rachel's sepulchre,...; and they will say unto thee, The asses which thou wentest to seek are found; and, lo, thy father hath left off caring for the asses, and is anxious for you,... ³Then shalt thou go on forward from thence, and thou shalt come to the oak of Tabor; and there shall meet thee there three men going up to God to Bethel, one carrying three kids, and another carrying three loaves of bread, and another carrying a bottle of wine: ⁴and they will salute thee, and give thee two loaves of bread, which thou shalt receive of their hand. ⁵After that thou shalt come to the hill of God, where is the garrison of the Philistines:..., when thou art come thither to the city, that thou shalt meet a band of prophets coming down*

from the high place with a psaltery, and a timbrel, and a pipe, and a harp, before them; and they will be prophesying: ⁶and the Spirit of Jehovah will come mightily upon thee, and thou shalt prophesy with them, and shalt be turned into another man [1 Samuel 10:2-6].

In this portion of Scripture, Samuel tells Saul that a specific sequence of events will occur after Samuel and Saul separate:

- When Saul leaves Samuel, Saul finds two men by Rachel's tomb who tell him that they have discovered his father's donkeys and that his father is now worried about Saul's whereabouts.
- When Saul comes to the plain of Tabor, he will meet three men going to Bethel to worship God. One man will carry three loaves of bread, one will have three kids, and one will hold a bottle of wine.
- The men will salute Saul and give him two loaves of bread.
- When Saul travels to the "Hill of God" [probably Gibeah, the town where Samuel lived], he will meet a company of prophets carrying musical instruments.
- As the prophets begin to prophesy, the Spirit of the Lord comes upon Saul.

1 Samuel 10:9 tells us that all these events occurred just as Samuel had described them. God spoke to Saul through Samuel about these future events so that Saul would know that Samuel spoke truthfully about God's calling him to be king of Israel.

Predictive or foretelling prophecies also occur throughout the New Testament. I previously mentioned one that Agabus prophesied to Paul. Let us now turn to Luke 2:28-35, where Simeon prophesied about Jesus to his parents.

²⁸*then he received him into his arms, and blessed God, and said,*

²⁹*"Now you are releasing your servant, Master, according to your word, in peace;* ³⁰*for my eyes have seen your salvation, ...* ³²*a light for revelation to the nations, and the glory of your people Israel."*

³⁴*and Simeon blessed them, and said to Mary, his mother, "Behold, this child is set for the falling and the rising of many in Israel, and for a sign which is spoken against.* ³⁵*Yes, a sword will pierce through your own soul, that the thoughts of many hearts may be revealed."*

³⁶*There was one Anna, a prophetess, the daughter of Phanuel, of the tribe of Asher (she was of a great age, having lived with a husband seven years from her virginity,* ³⁷*and she had been a widow for about eighty-four years), who didn't depart from the temple, worshiping with fastings and petitions night and day.* ³⁸*Coming up at that very hour, she gave thanks to the Lord, and spoke of him to all those who were looking for redemption in Jerusalem. [Luke 2:28-30, 32, 34-38, WEB].*

Note the specifics of what is prophesied here in Luke:

- Vs. 32—Simeon declares that Jesus will fulfill Isaiah 42:6. He will be a light to the Gentiles and the glory for Israel.
- Vs. 34—Simeon declares that Jesus will cause the fall and rising of many in Israel [see John 2.11]. Those who reject him [Isaiah 8:14; Matthew 21:42-44; Acts 4:11; Romans 9:33; 1 Corinthians 1:23] will fall; those who accept and receive him will rise—"be saved" [Zechariah 12-13:1; Romans 11:25-29; Acts. 15:13-15].
- Vs. 35—A sword would pierce Mary's soul [she would see Jesus crucified—John 19:25-27].
- Vs. 36-38—While the actual words of Anna [who was an acknowledged prophetess] are not recorded here in

Luke, her words confirmed Simeon's words. These two prophetic declarations fulfilled the legal requirements of the Law concerning legal testimony [Numbers 35:30; Deuteronomy 17:6; Matthew 18:15-20; 2 Corinthians 13:1].

Paul spoke of predictive prophecies concerning the end times in 1 Thessalonians 4:13-17, 2 Thessalonians 1:5-10, and 2:1-12. The final book in the New Testament, Revelation, foretells the end of this age and the final destruction of evil.

Declarative prophecies: forthtelling

The second type of prophecy, a "forthtelling word," does not focus on future events. In this type of prophecy, a prophet reveals why God is acting as He is in a particular circumstance or how God considers a current situation. This type of word reveals God's heart. Let's look at an example of forthtelling in the Old Testament. Turn to Jeremiah 9:23-24. Here, God speaks about man's attitudes and understanding of who God truly is. Let's read:

> ²³*Thus saith Jehovah, Let not the wise man glory in his wisdom, neither let the mighty man glory in his might, let not the rich man glory in his riches;* ²⁴*but let him that glorieth glory in this, that he hath understanding, and knoweth me, that I am Jehovah who exerciseth lovingkindness, justice, and righteousness, in the earth: for in these things I delight, saith Jehovah [Jeremiah 9:23-24].*

In the remainder of this chapter, God provides a predictive foretelling of His judgment on Egypt, Judah, Edom, Ammon, and Moab. However, to properly understand God's actions, you must first understand the true nature of God, as revealed in verses 23-24. Every time the Bible talks about God's love for His people, His compassion for the lost, or His strength

or power, that is a forthtelling prophecy [See Jeremiah 31:20; 32:40-41; Psalms 10:14, 17-18].

To summarize, we may say that prophecy is a message from God to a person [or donkey!] for that person to share with someone else. That message may provide information about the future or reveal God's heart and thoughts. Words of Knowledge[3] and Wisdom [two of the New Testament gifts of the Holy Spirit (see 1 Corinthians 12:1-11) often come forth during a forthtelling word from the Lord. Nonetheless, a prophecy is a message from God, whatever its form or format. If a message is not from God, it is not a prophecy, regardless of whether the message seems to come true or even if miracles accompany it.

A prophecy may provide information about the future or reveal God's heart and thoughts. However, prophetic ministry will not last forever, for men will not always need prophetic revelations. Both the New Testament and the Jewish Talmud declare that prophecy will come to an end. 1 Corinthians 13 states that while we now prophesy in part [v. 9], prophecy will be done away with when "the perfect" comes and we "know fully."

> [9]For we know in part, and we prophesy in part; [10]but when that which is perfect is come, that which is in part shall be done away [1 Corinthians 13:9-10].

Prophecy or Promise?

One final thought about what prophecy is and is not. A prophecy from the Lord is not the same as a promise from God. However, many prophecies, especially those foretelling prophetic words, refer to a future fulfillment, such as the expected fulfillment of promises.

The word "promise" comes from the Latin *promissa* and means "a declaration" or "verbal announcement" that one will do [or

not do] something or make [or not make] something happen. The result usually leaves the person under discussion with an advantage. The Old Testament word traditionally translated as "promise" is *DABAR*, which means "to talk, to utter, to pronounce" and usually refers to God's promises to and for Israel [Deuteronomy 1:11; 6:3; 9:23; 15:6]. The New Testament Greek word traditionally translated as "promise" is *epaggelia*. The root word aggelia means "something being announced." Some of the differences between promises and prophecies include:

- Promises relate to something that will bless or help a person or group. While prophecies often speak of blessings, they [especially Old Testament or end-time New Testament prophecies] may also mention possible judgments, trials, hardships, and persecutions.
- Promises tend to be addressed to groups, while prophecies may concern only one person.
- Promises may be fulfilled through multiple generations. See references to the "promises of the Father" or of "the Holy Spirit" [Luke 24:49; Acts 1:4; 2:33, 39; Galatians 4:14; Ephesians 1:13]. Prophecies often focus on specific times or individuals.
- All prophecy is conditional. Its fulfillment depends on the obedience and faith of the person receiving the prophecy [Nineveh repented, so Jonah's prophecy did not come to pass]. Promises will come to pass, even if one group of people loses the benefit of that promise because of their unbelief [the generation of Hebrews that left Egypt did not enter the Promised Land, but their children did].
- A prophecy may change into a promise through acts of faith and obedience. God prophesied to Abraham in Genesis 12:1-4; 13:14-17, established a covenant with him in Genesis 15 concerning Israel, established a more extensive covenant involving many nations in Genesis 17, and swore or promised to uphold the second more extensive covenant in Genesis 22:15-18.

Prophetic Song [The Song of the Lord]

Earlier, I wrote that prophecy could come through spoken words, dreams, visions, mime, or other symbolic actions. There is another specific type of prophecy—the "prophetic song" [also called "The Song of the Lord]." This is a type of prophecy sung to music or performed a cappella. This song is an inspired, anointed song that the Holy Spirit directs to be sung by an individual. It is a prophecy that is sung, not spoken [it is referred to in the New Testament as "spiritual songs" [See Colossians 3:16; Ephesians 5:19].

While the term "prophetic song" is not found in the Bible, the Book of Psalms records various prophetic songs ["the spiritual songs"] written by David and others. Moses sang a prophetic song [Deuteronomy 23], and Isaiah 5:1-7 may be a prophetic song. The prophet Habakkuk included a song of prophetic adoration at the end of his recorded prophecy. Most Bibles even include the written directive words, "To the choirmaster: with stringed instruments," at the end of the song in the passage we label Habakkuk 3:1-19. I have included part of that song here:

> [17]*For though the fig tree shall not flourish, Neither shall fruit be in the vines; The labor of the olive shall fail, And the fields shall yield no food; The flock shall be cut off from the fold, And there shall be no herd in the stalls:* [18]*Yet I will rejoice in Jehovah, I will joy in the God of my salvation.* [19]*Jehovah, the Lord, is my strength; And he maketh my feet like hinds' [feet], And will make me to walk upon my high places [Habakkuk 3:17-19].*

I previously mentioned that 1 Samuel 10:2-7 was a predictive prophecy concerning Saul. Do you remember that when he met the company of prophets, they were carrying musical

instruments? Although the passage does not explicitly state that they sang a prophetic song when they met Saul, it is possible that they did so. In 2 Kings 3:11-15, Elisha calls for music before prophesying to an evil king. While Elisha probably called for the music in preparation for speaking the Word of the Lord, did he say or sing his prophecy? The possibility exists that he sang.

The writer of Chronicles also infers that the Levites who were involved in the ministry at the temple ministered in the prophetic song [1 Chronicles 25:1-8]. In addition, Levitical music played by the Levites, as directed by the Holy Spirit, had an essential role in the wars of Israel. Prophetic music and song were recognized as a crucial spiritual weapon for the nation. 2 Chronicles 2:20-29 speaks of the singers going out before the armies of Judah under Jehoshaphat to face the coalition armies of Ammon, Moab, and Mount Seir. Their praise and worship songs probably involved singing prophetic declarations about God's goodness and foretelling God's control of the battle.

In the New Testament, prophetic songs have a distinct purpose in the life of the Church. Prophetic songs may occur spontaneously during worship services as the Holy Spirit responds or directs the congregation's worship. This song may arise from the worship leader or someone in the congregation.

During the prophetic song, the Holy Spirit may use known music [melodies recognized by the congregation or the person presenting the song], or the Spirit may introduce an original melody. This introduction of a new song might occur during a church service or during a time of personal meditation and worship. The Holy Spirit may also direct a person to sing a known song or psalm at a specific time for a prophetic reason. For example, during a service in which a beloved pastor was being released by the church body to pursue a call to overseas ministry, one of the intercessors was prompted to sing out a

well-known chorus from the 1980s with a slight change to the original words:

> *You shall go out with joy and be led forth with peace.*
> *The mountains and the hills will break forth before*
> *you.*
> *There'll be shouts of joy and all the trees of the field*
> *Will clap, will clap their hands.*
> *And all the trees of the field will clap their hands,*
> *The trees of the fields will clap their hands,*
> *The trees of the fields will clap their hands as you go*
> *out with joy [based on Isaiah 55:2].*

During intense intercession, the Holy Spirit may also introduce a prophetic song with warlike themes. When the Spirit introduces a warfare song, the music usually reflects the warfare theme by becoming staccato or march-like; tambourines and drums are often used.

Prophesy

Our third definition is for the word "prophesy." This word means "the act of giving a prophecy." It can be easy to mix up the English words "prophecy" and "prophesy," even though one is a noun, and the other is a verb. I sometimes mix up these words myself, but I have a way to keep the words separate in my mind. The word "prophecy" is a noun; "prophesy" is a verb. To talk or to say is an action; the action verb "prophesy" has an "s" just like the verb "says." When a prophet is giving a message from God, whether he or she speaks, sings, or acts out that word in a mime, he or she is prophesying. The "what" that he or she is speaking, acting out, or miming—the noun form [the name of the action]—is the prophecy.[4]

Prophets only prophesy when they speak God's words as the Holy Spirit directs them. Their divinely inspired words form the prophecy. While prophets may speak with great wisdom

at other times, they only prophesy when speaking under the leading and inspiration of the Holy Spirit [see 2 Peter 1:20-21].

Prophet

The last of the basic definitions in this lesson is for the word "prophet." Earlier, I wrote about how people's definition of "prophet" could be somewhat controversial. There are several ways to define the word "prophet," and people may have different ideas concerning what or who a prophet is. These differing ideas result from diverse teachings and general concepts associated with the term "prophet."

What image comes to mind when you think of the word "prophet?" Take a moment to think about that. Write down who or what you think a prophet is. Having a clear understanding of the definition of a prophet is essential. How you define the term "prophet" will influence your acceptance of prophetic ministry.

_____

_____

_____

What image came to mind while you wrote your definition of a prophet? Different people use the term "prophet" in various ways. Someone who studies the stock market and provides sound financial advice is often referred to as a financial guru or a financial prophet. Like Nostradamus, individuals who claim to know the future have been referred to as prophets. Islam also recognizes many biblical people as being prophetic.[5]

In contrast, while many claim the ability to prophesy and others consider certain people to be prophetic, only those called of the Lord were [or are] true prophets of God [Yahweh]. The actual Biblical prophet was a spokesman for God. He or she was chosen and commissioned by God [and nobody

else] to speak to an individual or group to convey or deliver a message or teaching.

In this book, I define the term "prophet" [and by extension "prophetess"] as men and women both of old and of today who reveal the heart of the true and only God as He discloses His purpose and plans to them.[6] I consider prophets to be only those who speak for the Triune God, consisting of the Father, the Son, and the Holy Spirit. All others are not true prophets.

In the Old Testament, the prophets were God's champions. They responded to God's call and demonstrated the personal relationship and trust God desired to have with His people. Like Enoch, these were the men and women who walked with God. In the New Testament, prophets are part of the Body of Christ, chosen and beloved by God [1 Colossians 3:12].

However, there are some who pretend to be prophets for various reasons, but who are not called by God and do not know Him. Throughout history, certain people have claimed to be prophets who do not believe in God or accept the Lord Jesus Christ as their Lord and Savior. <u>These so-called seers or prophets received their revelations from their personal thoughts or outside of God's legitimate sources.</u> I refer to these so-called prophets as either "pseudo prophets" or "spiritualists" [Hebrew calls these "KOSEM"]. According to the Bible, while many people claimed the ability to see the future, only those called by the Lord were true prophets. Remember that a true prophet is a spokesman [woman] who God has divinely commissioned to speak to a person or a people God's words or message.

Unfortunately, there are also those whom God has called to serve as His messengers who have fallen from their position, compromising or prostituting their calling. [These are more dangerous than the KOSEM.] 1 Kings 13:18, Nehemiah 6:12,

Jeremiah 23:25-27, and Lamentations 2:14 all reveal the damage a false or fallen prophet can cause.

The Bible warns us not to consider or be influenced by pseudo-prophets[7] or spiritualists and to evaluate the claims of those who state they are God's prophets. The New Testament warns us that

> [1]*Beloved, believe not every spirit, but prove the spirits, whether they are of God; because many false prophets are gone out into the world [1 John 4:1].*

I mentioned earlier that the Old Testament prophets established the standards for the entire community of Israel. Prophets in the Old Testament were role models of holiness and intimacy with God. Their anointing to prophesy came from God as He commissioned them to deliver His messages to humanity, especially Israel. These messages focused on five main areas:

- Prophecies revealing that God was speaking through the prophet[ess].
- Prophecies declaring that God wanted to create or maintain a relationship with the person or group of people.
- Prophecies proclaiming a person or people [usually Israel] had turned away from God [had broken their covenant with God].
- Prophecies warn that judgment will follow if the person or people do not repent [return to God by obeying Him]. These include prophecies concerning the judgment upon the nation and people of Israel.
- Prophecies assuring people that after God judged the people for their sin and disobedience, He would be merciful and send "a Messiah" who would restore and heal. These prophecies included those concerning the last days [the Day of the Lord].

Later New Testament prophets provide[d] wisdom, comfort, insight, and direction for the Body of Christ. However, in this Church age, the model for holiness is not Abraham or Moses and the Law but Jesus Christ, Who is the living embodiment of prophecy [Revelation 19:10] and the actual Word of God [John 1:1,14]. Nevertheless, whether a prophet received an Old Testament or a New Testament anointing, true prophets spoke [speak] or revealed [reveal] the heart of God as He disclosed [discloses] His purpose and plan. Thus, prophetic ministry's purpose focuses on <u>showing God's heart,</u> not the future.

Now, while it is beyond this course to do an exhaustive study of Hebrew or Greek, a short explanation of the Hebrew and Greek words for "prophet" can provide us some insight into who the prophets were [and are] and how their giftings operated [operate].

The standard, basic Hebrew word for prophet is "NABI" [or "NAVI"], which means "spokesman" or "speaker." Thus, NABI can be translated as a "person authorized to speak for another." The root of NABI, which means "to bubble forth," refers to the prophet's role as a speaker. The word NABI emphasizes the prophet as one called into service by God or who calls to men on behalf of God, revealing God's will to them. The term stresses the prophet's role as a speaker. 1 Samuel 3:20 states that Samuel was established as a NABI of the Lord, and Elijah was named a NABI prophet in 1 Kings 18:36.

However, two other Hebrew words refer to Old Testament prophets. The first word was HOZEH, and the second was RO'EH; both these terms are translated as "seer." In the Old Testament, the word seer [RO'EH][8] was first used to describe Samuel [1 Samuel 9:9]. Samuel was called a "seer" seven times. The second word, HOZEH, accentuates a person's ability to perceive events and their meaning, as well as the true nature

of another person's character and motivations. Both Hebrew words for "seer" can be found in the following Old Testament books:

- 1 Samuel 9:9, 11, 18-19
- 2 Samuel 24:11
- 2 Kings 17:13
- 1 Chronicles 9:22; 29:29
- 2 Chronicles 9:29; 12:15; 19:2; 29:30
- 2 Kings 17:13
- Isaiah 30:1
- Micah 3:7

The *NABI* prophet proclaimed God's message while the seer received a vision from God [Numbers 12:6, 8] and then shared his revelation [see Zechariah 1:7—6:14]. Both types of prophets spoke for God; they spoke in God's name and by His authority [Exodus 7:1]. The words they used were God's, not their own. In 1 Chronicles 29:29, all three words are used: Samuel the seer [*RO'EH*][8], Nathan the prophet [*NABI*], and Gad the seer [*HOZEH*].

Occasionally, prophets are referred to as messengers of God. The Hebrew word MAL'AK, which can also be translated as "angels" or "men of God," is used in these cases. "Man of God" was first used to describe Moses [Deuteronomy 33:1] and later used to refer to Samuel [1 Samuel 2:27; 9:6] and the unnamed "man of God" [1 Kings 13:1]. This phrase [2 Kings 4:9] denoted the people's recognition of the prophet's commitment to God. This designation was a term of respect, for the Hebrews recognized a difference in the character of the prophets of God. In 2 Kings 4:9, the Shunammite woman, referring to Elisha, states, *"I perceive that this is a holy man of God…"* The Old Testament also titles prophets as "the servants of God."

We must also note that the terms used to refer to the prophets can overlap in specific passages.

¹¹And when David rose up in the morning, the word of Jehovah came <u>unto the prophet Gad, David's seer</u>, saying, ¹²Go and speak unto David, Thus saith Jehovah, I offer thee three things: choose thee one of them, that I may do it unto thee." [2 Samuel 24:11-12. *Emphasis mine.*]

Other characteristics of prophets

A prophet is not necessarily a male. The Scriptures name seven female prophets. Other references refer to women who prophesy, like Phillip's daughters [Acts 21:9].

In the Old Testament, a prophet did not have to be a Jew, nor did the prophets always speak to Jews. Remember — Abraham was a Gentile [Deuteronomy 26:4-5]! Balaam was a Gentile prophet [Numbers 22] before he fell away, and some of the Jewish prophets, such as Jonah, were sent on missions to speak to the Gentiles. God even commissioned Elijah to anoint Hazael [a Gentile] to be king over Syria, a Gentile nation and enemy of Israel. [1 Kings 19:15][9].

Whoever they were, the prophets were inimitable individuals who carried a unique and solemn responsibility to the Lord.

⁶But if the watchman see the sword come, and blow not the trumpet, and the people be not warned, and the sword come, and take any person from among them; he is taken away in his iniquity, but his blood will I require at the watchman's hand. ⁷So thou, son of man, I have set thee a watchman unto the house of Israel; therefore hear the word at my mouth, and give them warning from me. ⁸When I say unto the wicked, O wicked man, thou shalt surely die, and thou dost not speak to warn the wicked from his way; that wicked man shall die in his iniquity, but

his blood will I require at thy hand. ⁹Nevertheless, if thou warn the wicked of his way to turn from it, and he turn not from his way; he shall die in his iniquity, but thou hast delivered thy soul [Ezekiel 33:6-9].

Prophets were and are warriors for God. They act as guardians of the covenant relationship between man and God. Remember, while they usually battled through intercession and prayer, Samuel and Elijah used real swords to slay the enemies of God [1 Samuel 15:32-33; 1 Kings 18:40]. New Testament prophets[10], operating under the Law of Grace, demonstrate the love of Jesus to people but fiercely war against spiritual wickedness [Ephesians 6:10-12, Acts 26:16-18] that seeks to weaken and destroy the Church.

The Prophetic Presbytery

The term "prophetic presbytery" does not appear in the Bible. In the Old Testament, however, references exist to "a company of prophets" ministering. The New Testament mentions groups of prophets ministering [Acts 13:1-3]. The term "prophetic presbytery" developed from the Greek word *presbyterion*, which refers to a group of elders or ministers. From this Greek word, we receive the English word "presbytery." Thus, a "prophetic presbytery" refers to a group of mature believers who gather at a specific time and place to provide prophetic ministry to an individual or a designated group.

In the Old Testament, the work of "a company of prophets" provided personal ministry to individuals and established people in their gifting or anointing [1 Samuel 10:5-16]. Other Biblical references indicate that interaction with a company of prophets results in unique, even life-changing experiences [1 Samuel 19:18-24; Numbers 11:16-29]. In the New Testament, the terminology of "company" or "sons of the prophets" is not used, for the "set-apart" state of the prophets no longer exists.

Instead, the emphasis is on "Body ministry" as the Church, the "Ecclesia," the "called out ones," is celebrated.

In the Acts of the Apostles and the subsequent books, the ministry of the Body of the Church is revealed. The Greek word *"presbyterion"*[11] refers to a group of ministers, including groups of elders or mature believers with demonstrable wisdom and Godly authority, ministering prophetically to strengthen individuals and the church. While this prophetic presbytery may be composed of people not formally recognized as prophets[12], the gathering can convey a personal prophecy. This prophetic presbytery can bring encouragement, clarity, and understanding to believers, as well as strength to the local church body.

Paul is recalling a meeting of a prophetic presbytery when he says to Timothy:

> [4]*Neglect not the gift that is in thee, which was given thee by prophecy, with the laying on of the hands of the presbytery [1 Timothy 4:14].*

Prophetic Acts

As stated before, most prophecies are spoken; some are sung. However, God sometimes calls upon His prophets to act out a prophecy. These actions are called prophetic acts. Prophetic acts involve specific actions, performed by a prophet, to convey God's message to an individual or group. These actions provide a visual explanation of what God is doing or will do.

Prophetic acts are unique in that they present a memorable, visual, and tactile representation of God's message to a group. God uses these prophetic acts to communicate His will and His love to humanity. Through these acts, God calls people to repentance and faithfulness; often, a prophetic act serves

as the final warning to avoid judgment. These specific actions demonstrated a divine judgment upon an individual or a particular group of people.

- Noah's building of the ark [Genesis 6] was an act of obedience but also served as a prophetic act. The great size of the ark and Noah's dedication to building it were a visual testimony of the serious nature of God's warning concerning the divine judgement of the flood.
- God commanded Hosea, the prophet, to marry Gomer, a prostitute [Hosea 1:2-Hosea 3]. Hosea's marriage and family life became a prophetic act revealing Israel's unfaithfulness to God.
- In the New Testament, when Jesus cursed the fig tree [Mark 11:12-14, 20-21], the shriveling of the tree at the Lord's words was a prophetic act that foretold the judgement on Israel the nation of Israel for their rejection of their Messiah.

Other prophetic acts enforce the seriousness of a prophetic word.

- Elisha had the king of Israel shoot arrows to demonstrate that God would give victory to Israel. However, the king's lack of understanding and trust kept him from receiving the fullness of God's blessing [2 Kings 13:15-19].
- Samuel's anointing of David was a prophetic act that demonstrated God's favor upon David [1 Samuel 16:1-13].

However, these acts, while impactful to the culture or group for which they are performed, may seem confusing to other groups. Today, when believers read the account of Jesus cursing the fig tree, they may not understand the connection between the fig tree and Israel. They may wonder why Jesus was so angry with a tree.

Conclusion and Summary

In this chapter, I have defined six terms we must grasp to understand God's purpose and plan for a revelatory, prophetic ministry. These terms are:

- Prophecy—a message from God. This message or revelation may involve foretelling the future or revealing God's perspective on the present. The importance of prophecy lies in the truth that it is a revelation of God's will and heart.
- Prophesy—the act of revealing or speaking God's heart to humanity.
- The Prophetic Song, also known as the Song of the Lord, is a prophecy conveyed through singing a song or speaking in time to music.
- Prophet and Prophetess—Men and women of old [and of today] who reveal the heart of the true and only God as He reveals His purpose and plans to them.
- Prophetic Presbytery—a united group of mature individuals who prophetically encourage believers and confirm a believer's gifts and ministries.
- Prophetic Acts—visual demonstrations or warnings that reveal God's will concerning a situation.

Having defined the various terms used in this book, we can now examine the development of prophetic ministry as outlined in the Bible and consider how and why God began to call certain men and women into the prophetic role. The unfolding story is a story of tragedy and triumph, failure and perseverance.

Endnotes for Chapter II: Definitions: A Plethora of Ps

¹Some translations will use the word "burden" or "prophecy"
for "oracle".

²I define "zombie" as someone who has lost all independent,
conscious thought and whose actions are controlled by
another's will.

³A word of knowledge is information gained supernaturally
through the Holy Spirit. This is information the person
could not know any other way. A word of wisdom is
how to use information and knowledge one has or how
to act in a delicate situation.

⁴This way of differentiating between "prophesy" and
"prophecy" may not work in other languages!

⁵However, the Islamic definition of is a prophet is different
from the definition accepted by people in relationship
with Jesus. The Moslems consider Mohammad to be
the Prophet [the last and greatest prophet] of Allah.
Jesus is viewed as a "inferior" prophet and not the Son
of God.

⁶There is a second part to this definition that we will consider
later. Because the prophet was willing to listen and
commune with God and to speak for God to others,
God was willing to listen when the prophet spoke about
others to God. Thus, we see the prophet often assumed
the mantle of the intercessor. See the following verses:
Genesis 18: 2-33—Abraham for the people of Sodom
Exodus 32:11-14—Moses for Israel
Lamentations 5:1-22—Jeremiah for fallen Judah

⁷Some were people God had called to be His prophets but fell
away because of their lusts.

⁸It appears from 1 Samuel 9:9 that "seer" [RO'EH] was the
older name for those who later were called "prophets."
This change may have resulted from the desire to
differentiate between Godly and pagan seers.

⁹There is no Biblical record that Elijah actually did this. Most
scholars believe that Elijah did not live to anoint Hazael

king of Syria himself. Instead, he sent his servant and successor Elisha to do this [2 Kings 8:9-15].

[10]In the Old Testament Era of the Kings, while Elijah was not the head of the Theocracy, he was a "government agent" acting to uphold the Law as given on Mount Sinai.

[11]Please note: In this book, I denote Hebrew words by using italicized capital letters. Greek words are italicized but not capitalized.

[12]These may be people with ministries inside or outside the church who also flow in the prophetic. Such people might include pastors, evangelists, medical doctors, mail carriers, homemakers, teachers, certified counselors, etc.

CHAPTER III

THE POWER OF THE WORD

The Wonder of Revelation

Before we continue our discussion, I would like to explore what theologians generally refer to as "general revelation". While we are discussing prophecy, I don't want you to think that prophetic ministry is the only way God reveals Himself. Our God longs for us to come to Him and fellowship with Him. Prophecy is only one of the ways that God reveals Himself to us.

God is continually revealing Himself because He wants us to know Him. He shows us that He is a God of beauty in His sunsets and sunrises, that He likes to laugh through the uniqueness of His Creation [look at the giraffe or the platypus], and that He is a caring healer [notice how our bodies fight off diseases, and injuries heal themselves]. He shows us that He is influential and trustworthy by protecting our planet and holding the universe together. [Scientists have discovered that the universe would have flown apart, except for something they call "dark matter" that holds it together]. The stars continually sing of His greatness as astronomers [who have discovered the universe is a noisy place], and the Bible reveals to us, though we may not understand the song. This testimony through nature is available to all men, even those who have never heard of Jesus Christ.

¹The heavens declare the glory of God;
And the sky showeth his handiwork.
²Day unto day uttereth speech,
And night unto night showeth knowledge [Psalm
19:1-2].

Prophecy is not valuable because it is unusual. The value of prophecy is that it reveals a portion of the Lord's will or His heart toward us. If a message or word does not indicate the Lord's heart and will to us, it isn't a true prophecy.

The Bible speaks of walking by "faith" and not by "sight" [2 Corinthians 5:7]. However, this walk of faith does not mean we can never intimately know God. The longer we walk with God, the greater our revelation of Him, and our faith grows stronger. We realize that God is too big to "know" [*ginosko¹*] entirely, but we can, to our delight, "know" [*ginosko*] and discover more about God each day [if we choose to pursue a closer relationship].

Prophetic ministry is only one of the ways [not the only way] that we can draw closer to God and learn more about what He is thinking and saying. Many people have come to a saving knowledge of our Lord and grown close to Him by studying the Bible. Another way to know God is through His providential care: my sister came to God after experiencing His loving care for her during a backpacking trip through Europe. Many written accounts describe the witness to God found in nature. God speaks and touches lives in many ways, and He is not limited to revealing His will and power through one method.

However, God has always chosen individuals to speak His words. We live in an exciting time today, when the prophetic ministry has emerged from obscurity. After a thousand years

42

of relative silence, prophets are again recognized and listened to in various Christian bodies.

In the Beginning: And God said

Now that we have briefly examined the general revelation of God available to humankind and defined a basic understanding of prophecy, prophecy, prophet, prophetic presbytery, and the Song of the Lord, we can begin to focus on our study. To start, we turn to the book of beginnings, Genesis.

The first book of the Bible, Genesis, derives its name from the Greek word meaning "birth," "beginnings," or "origin." In this book, God has given us a grand overview of the Creation, man's beginnings, and the origin of sin. Here, in the first three chapters of Genesis, the seeds of all the essential teachings of the Bible are first planted. In other chapters of the Genesis, we discover the keys to identifying many of the peoples and nations named in later prophecies.

Genesis 1 and 2 reveal that Adam and Eve were made in the image of God. This statement meant that, like God, Adam and Eve possessed a spiritual nature and could reason and choose. God created the man and the woman to have both a spiritual and an earthly nature, so that they could be rulers over the earth, "keepers" of the garden, and stewards of creation. In their very essence, Adam and Eve were living prophetic ambassadors of God, for they were God's representatives standing before all of creation.[2]

The life and being of Adam and Eve, as they lived in harmony and unity with each other and with the Godhead, were to be a revelation of God's purpose and love to all of creation. They represented God's power and love through their care and protection of the garden.

So let us take a moment to reread those familiar first words that open the Genesis account:

> *In the beginning, God created the heavens and the earth. ²And the earth was waste and void; and darkness was upon the face of the deep: and the Spirit of God moved upon the face of the waters. ³And God said, Let there be light: and there was light [Genesis 1:1-3].*

Buried within the familiar words of this opening chapter of Genesis, prophetic principles emerge in their "baby" forms.

- God's words have power. When God speaks, His words have creative power. In Genesis 1, we see that each time God speaks, a creative, innovative process occurs:

  > *And God said, Let there be light: and there was light.... ⁶And God said, Let there be a firmament in the midst of the waters,... ⁷And God made the firmament,... and it was so.... ⁹And God said, Let the waters under the heavens be gathered together unto one place, and let the dry land appear: and it was so [Genesis 1:3, 6,7, 9. Emphasis mine].*

  Later, we discover in the New Testament that the continuing existence of the universe is the result of the Word of God [Jesus] holding all things together [Colossians 1:15,17].

- God's words change reality. The Spirit moves and acts when the Triune God, the Elohim, speaks. We can recognize that the Spirit of God is moving because a creative, transforming word comes forth [see Genesis 1:2b].

- God's words are creative. God's words always have creative, transforming power. His word does not return to Him without accomplishing what He wants it to accomplish [see Isaiah 55:11-12].
- God speaks with purpose. God was speaking creative, transforming words before man appeared on the earth. God does not need a human being to speak His word for His words to have power. It is a privilege for any person to declare or demonstrate God's words. God gave the various forms of prophetic ministry as an act of kindness and grace.

Most commentators agree that Genesis 3:15 is God's first and most crucial prophecy. The rest of the Bible unfolds God's plan for man's redemption. However, before turning to Chapter Three, we must examine the statements in Genesis 1:26-27 and 2:15-17, for these statements have definite prophetic overtones.

> *26And God said, Let us make man in our image, after our likeness: and let them have dominion over the fish of the sea, and over the birds of the heavens, and over the cattle, and over all the earth, and over every creeping thing that creepeth upon the earth. 27And God created man in his own image, in the image of God created he him; male and female created he them [Genesis 1:26-27. Emphasis mine].*

> *15And Jehovah God took the man, and put him into the garden of Eden to dress it and to keep it. 16And Jehovah God commanded the man, saying, Of every tree of the garden thou mayest freely eat: 17but of the tree of the knowledge of good and evil, thou shalt not eat of it: for in the day that thou eatest thereof thou shalt surely die [Genesis 2:15-17. Emphasis mine].*

In Genesis 1:26, God declares that He will make man in His image. Man will be patterned after or created as a mirror reflection of God. He would also have God's likeness, with similar traits and potential. Only God Himself could make man resemble God! However, the verb forms of the Hebrew translated as, *"Let us make..."* in Genesis 1:26 and *"God made..."* in Genesis 1:27 are both in the *Qal* imperfect form.

Understanding what having a *Qal* form of a verb is essential. Simply put, using a *Qal* imperfect form means that the action involving the verb "make" is an incomplete, habitual, or customary[3] action. In other words, when God formed Adam and breathed the breath of life into him and then later formed Eve, these first humans were not the finished "products" that God desired for them to be. Think about that for a moment. Adam and Eve were not complete; in some critical way, they did not fully reflect God's image. [Notice that God did not specifically pronounce Adam or the Woman "good"]. What do you think was missing?

Genesis 1:31 states that God looked at everything He had made and saw that everything was "good." Genesis 2:2 states that God finished His work and rested on the seventh day [which became the Sabbath]. Yet the imperfect verb form of the Hebrew indicates that, in some way, Adam and Eve were unfinished. Thus, man was "good" but unfinished. We seem to have a contradiction, so let us look again at Genesis 2:16-17:

> *And Jehovah God commanded the man, saying, Of every tree of the garden thou mayest freely eat:* [17]*but of the tree of the knowledge of good and evil, thou shalt not eat of it: for in the day that thou eatest thereof thou shalt surely die"* [Genesis 2:16-17].

Adam and Eve lived in a perfect environment. There was only one rule to obey: do not eat of the tree of the knowledge of good and evil. That rule existed to create a simple test that

would put the final "polish" or "temper"[4] on their character: Would humankind choose to obey God and demonstrate their love and trust in their Creator by following this simple rule? Would they turn away from their Creator and please themselves? This test of obedience would reveal the true character of both the woman and the man when they were under stress. God's warning of the consequences that faced them has strong prophetic overtones: if either the male or female chose to eat the forbidden fruit, they would die.

Hope amid darkness

Unfortunately, neither Adam nor Eve passed the test of obedience. The aftermath of Adam and Eve's disregard for God's rule is recorded in Genesis 3, with Adam and Eve first hiding from God and then deflecting blame. Still, God's declaration recorded in Genesis 1:26 remains in force. God will make man in His image; man will become a true reflection and representative of the living God.

God's words in Genesis 3:9-23 are both an assertion of the consequences that man had brought upon himself and God's plan for removing those curses and bringing the promise in Genesis 1:26 to pass. God's purpose for humanity will be fulfilled.

- The snake would crawl on his belly and eat dust—a constant reminder to Satan that he would be ultimately defeated, and his rebellious pride would result in his complete humiliation. [See Ezekiel 28:17-19.]
- A continual war would exist between the serpent and the woman. While many women hate snakes, the real battle is the spiritual battle between Satan and the "woman" [Eve represents both the one who would bear the Lord Jesus and the Church]. [See Genesis 3:15, Revelation

12:1-6, Ephesians 5:22-32. See "Satan's seed" in Galatians 3:26-29, John 8:39-41, Ephesians 6:10-12.]

- Jesus, the Seed of Eve, would be bruised but would crush Satan and bring ultimate victory and restoration [Genesis 3:15].

Notice that in chapters one through three of Genesis, God reveals His eternal plan using symbols and prophetic language. As mentioned in the last chapter, the meaning of a prophecy often has several layers. God physically made man in Genesis 1:27, yet Adam was not yet "finished" because his character had not yet been tested. The first man failed his test, but God's plan to redeem humanity and fulfill the promise in Genesis 1:26 remained. God's original purpose for humanity will be fulfilled.

Genesis 3:15, which foreshadows Jesus' death on the Cross, is known as the *Protoevangelium*, which means "first Gospel". In this verse, the struggle between Satan and the woman's seed foreshadowed the ultimate defeat of Satan by Jesus' sacrificial death on the cross. However, this prophecy also foreshadows the struggle of righteous people against the power and influence of Satan in the years preceding Jesus' birth and in the period that now exists between Jesus' resurrection and Satan's final defeat [Revelation 20]. God is still forming the image of Christ, the second Adam, in us so that we may become like Jesus. The Holy Spirit is actively working in us so that we can fully establish God's will in our own lives and the areas of authority He desires to delegate to us.

The hope of the *Protoevangelium* is emphasized in Genesis 3, when God does a prophetic act for Adam and Eve. Although they had lost the glory and righteousness God had bestowed on them[5] and become naked [Genesis 3:7], He killed an animal and clothed them in the animal's hide [Genesis 3:21]. This act of God's foreshadowed the atonement that Israel would

receive through animal sacrifices and the final, more perfect atonement that all humanity can receive by faith through the blood of Jesus [Hebrews 10:1-23].

Thus, while Genesis only hints at much of the revelation of God's plan, we see that from the time of creation to Adam and Eve's expulsion from the garden, the voice of God was speaking with transformative power and authority. The voice of God spoke of future events even before the creation of man and continued to speak after the fall of man. Adam and Eve would share many of those words with their offspring as they longed for restoration to their garden home.

Exactly how God communicated with Adam and Eve or humanity before the time of the flood is not recorded in Genesis. Genesis merely states that God spoke to them. Originally, God may have chosen to walk with Adam and Eve in the early mornings, late afternoons, and evenings [Genesis 3:8] while speaking and communicating with them verbally at any time.

However, sin disrupted this fellowship. The communication between God and humanity was never the same, for sin and its shame made it difficult for men to face God. However, even after Adam and Eve sinned and hid from God, they could still speak directly with Him when they sought to do so [Genesis 3:8-11].

Nevertheless, the guilt, fear, and shame brought by sin made Adam and Eve want to conceal their inner thoughts from God even when they were talking with Him [Genesis 3:13-21]. Once sin entered, meeting with God evoked feelings of fear and dread within people [Genesis 3:8-10. See also Genesis 28:17; Exodus 20:18-21][6]. Therefore, after God comes to confront Adam and Eve in Genesis 3:8, we do not have any record of His "walking" with any man regularly except for Enoch [who

walked with God in a way that echoed the fellowship that God once had with Adam], before God "took" Enoch.

In Enoch, God found the same loving companionship with a person that He had enjoyed with Adam and Eve before they sinned. How could Enoch have such a unique fellowship with God when God told Moses that no one could see His glory and live?

- When God walked with Enoch, He set aside His glory and appeared in human form [this is called a "theophany" of God] so Enoch would not be incinerated.
- God handcrafted Man [Adam and Eve]; their physical bodies were perfect and were designed to last forever. Once man sinned, the slow process of the body decaying began, not only in individuals but throughout the entire race. This decay process slowly accelerated over centuries as DNA mutations lead to shorter lifespans. The human body became weaker. However, since Enoch lived only seven generations after Adam, his physical frame was more robust and resistant than that of modern humans.
- Enoch's hunger and thirst to know God involved a penitent attitude. His faith and trust enabled him to stand in the presence of God. [See Isaiah 6.]

During the earliest days recorded in Genesis, people's hearts had not hardened to the point where they could no longer hear God. Their spiritual ears were not yet dull, and men generally could not ignore God's voice. Thus, the Bible records that God spoke directly to righteous Enoch, Noah, and even a rebellious Cain in the depths of his sin. Cain, fresh with the blood of Abel on his hands, argued with God [Genesis 4].

However, communication between God and humanity deteriorated. Each rebellious choice made it more difficult for people to hear God's voice. Each disobedience caused

humanity to experience more guilt, shame, and fear of the loving but righteous God. When men began routinely ignoring God and disobeying Him, God found one man, Noah, who would still listen and converse with God. God chose Noah to carry His warning to humanity. Noah courageously testified of God's goodness and warned the people of a coming judgment [2 Peter 2:5] through a worldwide flood [Genesis 6:13-7:5].

Second rebellion

Unfortunately, humanity ignored both Noah's verbal warning and his shipbuilding. Ignoring God led to the judgment of the flood. Genesis 6-9 speaks of the destruction of all who would or could not listen to God's words. Only Noah, who heard God and followed His commands, and his family were saved. When Noah and his family departed from the ark, God established the Noahic covenant with the people and gave them the rainbow as the sign of this new covenant. However, as with the first covenant God had made with Adam, this Noahic covenant came with a test. This second test was to spread out over the earth.

Again, humanity failed the test of loving obedience to God. The unified decision of Noah's offspring to build a tower in defiance of God's will [see Genesis 11] led to God's confusing the people's languages. This act led to the formation of distinct languages and sowed the seeds of distrust between the various branches of the human family. A sadder result of this overt rebellion was a wider chasm between people and God. This chasm made it even more difficult for most people to hear the voice of God speaking to them. In general, most of the people groups attempted to appease God's [or the false gods'] wrath and avoided fellowshipping with Elohim.

The judgment of the flood temporarily slowed the effects of sin upon Creation but did not remove sin from either humanity or the earth. Therefore, God chose special individuals to speak

on His behalf and call humanity back to Him. These people were the prophets.

End Notes Chapter III: The Power of the Word

[1]The Greek word *"ginosko"* or "know" has many meanings, including to be aware of, to feel, and to understand. The word is also a Jewish idiom for sexual intercourse.

[2]God is spirit; humankind was a type of bridge composed of both spirit and earth.

[3]Genesis shows that creation was a one-time event, not a "customary" or "habitual" action. God is always creative, but the creation story was a distinct occurrence in time and space.

[4]Blacksmiths use fire to soften metals for shaping and a final "quenching" to make tools strong and blades extremely sharp. Our trials and tests as believers have the same purpose: *"We are His workmanship..."* [Ephesians. 2:10].

[5]Many scholars believe that Adam and Eve had been dressed in robes of righteousness before they sinned.

> *I will greatly rejoice in Yahweh!*
> *My soul will be joyful in my God,*
> *for he has clothed me with the garments of salvation.*
> *He has covered me with the robe of righteousness,*
> *as a bridegroom decks himself with a garland*
> *and as a bride adorns herself with her jewels [Isaiah 61:10,*
> *WEB. See also Colossians 3:5-14; Ephesians 4:24].*

[6]Remember what David wrote in Psalm 51: 1-17.

> *Have mercy upon me, O God, according to thy lovingkindness: According to the multitude of thy tender mercies blot out my transgressions.*
>
> *2Wash me thoroughly from mine iniquity, And cleanse me from my sin.*

3For I know my transgressions; And my sin is ever before me.

4Against thee, thee only, have I sinned, And done that which is evil in thy sight;

That thou mayest be justified when thou speakest, And be clear when thou judgest.

5Behold, I was brought forth in iniquity; And in sin did my mother conceive me.

6Behold, thou desirest truth in the inward parts; And in the hidden part thou wilt make me to know wisdom.

7Purify me with hyssop, and I shall be clean: Wash me, and I shall be whiter than snow.

8Make me to hear joy and gladness, That the bones which thou hast broken may rejoice.

9Hide thy face from my sins, And blot out all mine iniquities.

10Create in me a clean heart, O God; And renew a right spirit within me.

11Cast me not away from thy presence; And take not thy holy Spirit from me.

12Restore unto me the joy of thy salvation; And uphold me with a willing spirit.

13Then will I teach transgressors thy ways; And sinners shall be converted unto thee.

14Deliver me from bloodguiltiness, O God, thou God of my salvation; And my tongue shall sing aloud of thy righteousness.

15O Lord, open thou my lips; And my mouth shall show forth thy praise.

16For thou delightest not in sacrifice; else would I give it: Thou hast no pleasure in burnt-offering.

17The sacrifices of God are a broken spirit: A broken and a contrite heart, O God, thou wilt not despise.

CHAPTER IV

THE FIRST PROPHET

Abraham was the first person specifically named "a prophet" in the Scriptures[1]. Why does the Lord call Abraham a prophet? Why does the title of prophet first come into the biblical record at this time? The implication in Genesis is that while God was still speaking, still reaching out to humanity [see Genesis 20:3], most people had lost the ability to hear God's voice. As the downward spiral of sin continued impacting humankind, the ability or desire of most men [and women] to hear and listen to the voice of God grew weaker.

Nine chapters later [Genesis 20], when God warns Abimelech that Sarah is married, God spoke to the king in a dream, not directly to him face-to-face. Abimelech probably could not have heard God speaking either audibly or to His spirit while he [Abimelech] was awake, for his heart was not open to God. This account marked a turning point. Throughout the remaining pages of Scripture, as daily concerns filled people's conscious minds with apprehension and emotions, prophetic dreams and the prophets' declarations gained importance. When man's sensitivity to the Lord's voice waned and the siren call of sin grew louder, God began speaking to humanity's unconscious minds through dreams[2] and to their conscious minds through the mouths of His prophets.

Unfortunately, many chose not to listen to the prophets. Zechariah later declared that men deliberately choose to ignore God's voice.

But they refused to hearken and pulled away the shoulder, and stopped their ears, that they might not hear. ¹²Yea, they made their hearts as an adamant stone, lest they should hear the law, and the words which Jehovah of hosts had sent by his Spirit by the former prophets. [Zechariah 7:11-12a. Emphasis mine]

The Proto-prophets—the Patriarchs

With the call of God to Abraham at the beginning of Genesis 12, a beam of light begins to shine into the darkness of the soul of man. Out of all the people, God chose to call Abram [who became Abraham]. Why? Had others refused God's call? Was Abraham the only person left who could hear God's voice and desired to respond to His call?

> *¹Now Jehovah said unto Abram, Get thee out of thy country, and from thy kindred, and from thy father's house, unto the land that I will show thee: ²and I will make of thee a great nation, and I will bless thee, and make thy name great; and be thou a blessing: ³and I will bless them that bless thee, and him that curseth thee will I curse: and in thee shall all the families of the earth be blessed. ⁴So Abram went, as Jehovah had spoken unto him… [Genesis 12:1-4a].*

God chose Abraham to father a people who would have a unique relationship with Him. He wanted all other nations to understand by watching Israel that a relationship with God would bring peace, prosperity, and healing. This relationship between God and Israel would be built on God's grace and mercy and Israel's trust and obedience.

When God spoke to Abram [who became Abraham], He called Abram into a life of faith. How God talked to Abraham

is not recorded. He might have spoken to Abraham through an audible or inward voice, dreams, or visions. However, the impact of God's voice was such that Abraham abandoned his previous way of life, took his wife and worldly goods, and began his walk of obedience.

Why does the Lord call Abraham a prophet? No prophetic writings attributed to Abraham are known to exist. No miracles performed by Abraham are recorded. We have no direct records of Abraham foretelling the future or forthtelling God's purposes to those around him, except in his comment to Isaac[3]. However, Abraham fulfilled his prophetic call by:

- Choosing to believe God — Abraham believed God enough to uproot his family and follow God [Genesis 12:4]. This act of departing from his home to seek a new country may be considered a prophetic act. First, he demonstrated by his actions that God was trustworthy and worthy of obedience, just as Noah had previously done in building the ark. Second, his actions foretell future events. God intervened in Abraham's life, delivering Sarah out of Pharaoh's harem and having Pharaoh send Abraham away with all his goods [Genesis 12:10-20]. Later,

  o Israel will be led out of Egypt by Moses through God's power.
  o Jesus, by His death and resurrection, would bring those who followed Him out of sin and death.

- Acting in faith—Abraham walked the land, trusting God to give it to him [Genesis 13:14-18]. He rescued Lot, believing God would enable him to win against enormous odds [Genesis 14]. Abraham believed in God's Word that Isaac would be born, even though he and Sarah were too old to have a child. [Genesis 15; 17:1-21].

- Declaring a forthtelling word—After God changed His and his wife's names, Abraham prophesied of God's purposes by calling his wife "Sarah" instead of "Sarai" [See Genesis 17].
- Teaching his children—God chose Abraham, knowing that Abraham would faithfully teach his children. Abraham recounted the prophetic words that God spoke about the future of Israel to his children [Genesis 18:19].
- Developing a relationship with God—Abraham was willing to establish an intimate relationship with God. Because of that intimate relationship, God spoke to Abraham about the judgment facing Sodom and Gomorrah [Genesis 18:20-33].
- Acting as an Intercessor—Abraham pleaded with God to spare the innocent found in Sodom and Gomorrah [Genesis 18:22-33]. A fundamental part of a prophet's role is to stand as an intercessor before the Lord, as we shall see.

The children of Abraham, who descended through Isaac, inherited the prophetic mantle from their father, Abraham. While little is written of Isaac's relationship with God [he did speak a prophetic blessing over his sons], we know that Jacob talked with God [Genesis 28:11-22] and even wrestled with the Angel of the Lord [Genesis 32:23-30]. Jacob also proclaimed specific, detailed prophecies over his sons before his death [Genesis 48 and 49]. Jacob's favorite son, Joseph, became known as a dreamer and interpreter of dreams. His ability to interpret God-sent dreams saved his family, the people of Egypt, and others from famine. Joseph also gave a foretelling word, commanding that his bones be removed from Egypt when the Israelites returned to Canaan [Genesis 50:22-26].

Abraham's offspring

Abraham's descendants demonstrate the humanity of the Old Testament prophets. Their lives were not perfect. Isaac favored his oldest son, although he knew Esau was not spiritually minded. Jacob willingly deceived his father to usurp his blessing [Genesis 27:1-29]. Although Jacob desired God's blessings, he did not fully trust the Lord until he had grown old [Genesis 43:14; 46]. Joseph began life as a spoiled son who lacked wisdom. The lives of all twelve of the patriarchs [the sons of Jacob, including Joseph] demonstrated the need to grow from selfishness into maturity.

All the patriarchs struggled to trust God and walk in obedience to His Word, and some failed the test. [Judah's conduct for Tamar as recorded in Genesis 38 is just one such example.] However, while they often faltered, the Patriarchs held fast to the four promises[4] God gave Abraham and taught those promises to their children. Thus, God chose these ordinary men to be His representatives and the ancestors of Jesus Christ.

Summary

The book of Genesis makes it clear that God declared He would make humanity in His image, able to commune with the Godhead. Man [both the male and the female together] was to be God's prophetic representative to the physical creation. However, Adam and Eve's sin separated humanity from God and began a downward spiral that was only temporarily interrupted by the judgment of the flood.

Nevertheless, God was not surprised by man's failure to obey. As part of God's plan for redemption, He began to raise up men and women who would convey His love and message to humanity. The first of the prophets named in the Scriptures was Abraham. Through Abraham and his descendants, God

continued to speak out His love, even as the darkness of sin and idolatry increased, and men chose to close their hearts to the truth.

Endnotes Chapter IV: The First Prophet

[1]Prophets may have existed before this time. We do know from Jude and 2nd Peter that the Hebrews considered Enoch a prophet.

[2]Today many people in the Middle East are converting to Christianity after Jesus appeared to them in dreams.

[3]See Abraham's explanation to Isaac when Abraham was planning to sacrifice Isaac in obedience to God's command:

And Abraham said, God will provide himself the lamb for a burnt-offering, my son: so they went both of them together [Genesis 22:8].

[4]God promised Abraham that he would receive land, a great name, and children and that Abraham would be a blessing that would extend to the nations. [See Genesis 12 and Hebrews 11:9].

CHAPTER V

THE THEOCRACY OF ISRAEL

Introduction

Having closed the Book of Genesis and opened the Book of Exodus, we see God commissioning Moses to speak on His behalf and deliver an entire people from Egypt. Although hesitant at first, Moses delivered God's directives and eventually led the Theocracy [a theocracy is a God-centered government] that God established with Israel. This theocracy would operate from the time of the Exodus until the anointing of Saul as the King of Israel. During this period, God Himself would select a person to lead the people. The person designated by God would be responsible for enforcing the provisions of the covenant that God established with Israel.

Moses was the first leader of the Theocracy, and Samuel was the Theocracy's last leader. Looking at this period from the outside, we might consider the Theocracy a failure. The two best-known prophets of this Theocracy were Moses and Samuel, yet even these two men, influential as they were, faced opposition and disobedience at various times from the Hebrew people. During the time of the Theocracy, the disorganization of the tribes increased when various tribes ignored the teachings of the Law. However, when those tribes disobeyed God, Israel experienced the curses Moses had

foretold [Deuteronomy 11:26-28], resulting in years of turmoil and warfare.

Throughout the time of Theocracy, when the people cried out because of hardships, God blessed them with prophets and other leaders who led them into periods of renewal and prosperity. However, when this God-given leader [or judge] died, the people tended to forget the Law. Israel would again fall under a curse. Thus, a cycle of rebellion, oppression, repentance, deliverance, prosperity, and then more failure was created and repeated until the time of Samuel. Although Samuel was faithful to God, when Samuel grew old, the people demanded that Samuel appoint a king to make Israel like "other nations." The appointment of Saul as king ended the Theocracy.

Moses: A Heart on Fire

Let us back up for a moment to the beginnings of the Theocracy and the development of the confederation of Hebrew tribes into an independent nation. During this pivotal time in Israel's history as a nation, Moses spoke for God, conveying God's will to Pharaoh and the people of Israel. Moses gave the Law to Israel in its moral, ceremonial, and civic forms as God dictated it to him. [As part of that Law, which was itself a unique prophetic statement from God, Moses gave directives about prophecy and the treatment of prophets that stir controversy even today.] Finally, Moses foreshadowed the coming of the greatest prophet, the One Who was more than a prophet, Jesus Christ.

However, when God first confronted Moses at the burning bush, Moses was not interested in being God's ambassador or His prophet. Moses argued with God and was initially so lax in observing and fulfilling the requirements of the Abrahamic covenant that God almost killed him at "the incident at the Inn" [Exodus 4:24-26], as we shall see.

Yet God captured this reluctant leader's heart, and Moses became transfixed. When did this remarkable transformation take place? The Bible does not clearly say. The Exodus record, written by Moses himself, does not record Moses' thoughts. However, the grumbling, half-hearted, reluctant man who departed for Egypt was not the same man who later desperately sought God's presence and asked to see God's glory [Exodus 33:14-16a, 17-18].

Let us take a moment to examine Moses' initial interactions with God. Although God had providentially spared Moses' life [Exodus 2], Moses had never spoken with God or received a prophetic word from Him before encountering God at the burning bush. When God commissioned Moses to go to Pharaoh [Exodus 3:10-4:17], Moses gave excuses and attempted to decline the commission. He did not wish to deliver God's words to anyone.

> *And Moses said unto God, Who am I, that I should go unto Pharaoh, and that I should bring forth the children of Israel out of Egypt? [Exodus 3:11]*
>
> *[12] And Moses answered and said, But, behold, they will not believe me, nor hearken unto my voice; for they will say, Jehovah hath not appeared unto thee [Exodus 4:1].*
>
> *[13] And he said, Oh, Lord, send, I pray thee, by the hand of him whom thou wilt send [Exodus 4:13].*

Moses' attitude reminds me of a small child looking for reasons not to pick up his toys after he finishes playing with them. God showed immense patience with Moses' attitude [which seemed somewhat whiny]. God even assigned Aaron to Moses [Exodus 4:14-17] to act as Moses' spokesman.

Nevertheless, even when Moses did begin moving in obedience to the Word of God, his casual, half-hearted obedience almost cost him his life. As Moses journeyed toward Egypt, God confronted him at an unidentified inn and nearly killed him because Moses had not fulfilled the requirements of the Abrahamic covenant.

> On the way at a lodging place, Yahweh met Moses and wanted to kill him. ²⁵Then Zipporah took a flint, and cut off the foreskin of her son, and cast it at his feet; and she said, "Surely you are a bridegroom of blood to me."
> ²⁶So he let him alone. Then she said, "You are a bridegroom of blood," because of the circumcision [Exodus 4:24-26, WEB].

Obedience Is Mandatory

This curious incident contains a vital truth: <u>Those called into prophetic ministry must never forget that they serve a holy and righteous God. God sets the standard and the requirements</u> for those He chooses as His representatives. God's perspective is much different than ours.

> For my thoughts are not your thoughts, neither are your ways my ways, saith Jehovah. ⁹For as the heavens are higher than the earth, so are my ways higher than your ways, and my thoughts than your thoughts [Isaiah 55:8-9].

As a prince in the Egyptian court, Moses was raised in an atmosphere where his wishes were rarely questioned. When called by God, Moses freely expressed his reluctance to obey. Although Moses had finally acquiesced to God's directive, Moses had never obeyed the requirement that all of Abraham's male offspring be circumcised [Genesis 17:1-14]. Since Moses had never circumcised his son, he was not

in proper covenantal standing with the Lord. Only the drastic actions of Zipporah, his wife, saved Moses' life. Moses learned the necessity of obedience and appropriate fear of the Lord at the inn [the lodging place].

Centuries after Moses, King David, who loved God passionately, sought to honor God by bringing the Ark of the Covenant, which had been supernaturally restored to Israel after its capture by the Philistines [1 Samuel 6:1-12], up to David's new capital at Jerusalem. However, David neglected God's directive that only the Levites were to carry the ark. David had the ark placed on a cart drawn by oxen. When the oxcart hit a bump, and the ark became unstable, Uzzah put out his hand to balance the ark and was instantly killed [2 Samuel 6:1-9; 1 Chronicles 15:1-16:1]. God understood the good intentions of David's heart, but He needed David and the rest of Israel to realize that He is the One, True God, and His way of "doing things" was the only right and correct way. <u>Man can never elevate his ideas above the Lord's.</u>

In the examples I have given, both David and Moses acted presumptively[2]. However, perfect obedience to God's commands is what leads to success. Disobedience, partial obedience, or presumption can lead to tragedy. David learned that while God loved him, he was not above God's Law. David had to follow the commandment for the Levites to carry the ark when taking the ark to Jerusalem. Centuries before David lived, Moses had to learn the same lesson: Only complete obedience will be blessed[3].

From Obedience to Intimacy

From this incident at the inn through all the events in Egypt, Moses' understanding of God's greatness, his awe of God, and his trust in God continued to grow as God revealed His glory and power through the plagues that attacked Egypt. Aaron had to speak on behalf of Moses during their first encounters

with Pharaoh [Exodus 5:1-4]. However, as Moses obeyed God by confronting Pharaoh, God gave him the revelation of His Name, *"I AM THE LORD"* [Exodus 6:6-8]. When the children of Israel were too discouraged to listen to Moses' prophecy, Moses received and believed the Word. As the plagues continued, Moses spoke God's directives to Aaron, and Aaron acted out the prophetic judgments [See Exodus 7:9-12, 7:19-21, 8:1-2, 12-13]. However, when the fourth plague, the plague of flies occurred, God spoke directly to the Pharaoh through Moses. While Aaron still accompanied Moses, Aaron was now a silent witness; Moses was addressing Pharaoh himself. In the sixth plague of boils and blisters, Moses sprinkled the ashes that led to the formation of the boils. The seventh plague of hail, the eighth plague of locusts, and the ninth plague of darkness all were the result of Moses' prophetic actions. Then, in the final encounter between Pharaoh and Moses [Exodus 10:24-29], Aaron was not mentioned as even being present.

Moses saw a faithful God deliver the Israelites from the power of Egypt. He saw how the angel of death destroyed the firstborn of Egypt but spared those who were obedient to place the lamb's blood on their doorposts and lintels. Moses saw the Lord open the sea for Israel to pass through. Moses also saw God destroy the chariots of Egypt, which had attempted to pursue Israel. Moses experienced God's faithfulness in bringing the people to Mount Sinai.

When Moses returned to Mt. Sinai, he knew the power and majesty of his God. He knew Yahweh was the Lord. The drastic change in Moses' heart and mind was evident when Israel camped at Mount Sinai.

God had called Israel to Mt. Sinai to fulfill His Word to Abraham [Genesis 15:13-16] and to establish a unique relationship with Abraham's children. Israel was to be a nation of prophets, a people who, through their lives, worship, and words, would reveal the holiness and love of God to all the

nations that surrounded Israel.[4] At Mt. Sinai, the children of God were allowed to give themselves wholeheartedly to the God of their Fathers as God's holy priests and ambassadors to the nations.

The Tragedy of Israel

However, the interaction at Mt. Sinai dramatized the tragedy of Israel. While thankful to God for His blessings, the Hebrews drew back from the presence of the Lord. The people had declared, *"All that the LORD has spoken we will do"* [Exodus 19:8]. However, they later drew back and said to Moses, *"Speak with us, and we will hear, but do not let God speak with us, lest we die"* [Exodus 20:16; see also Exodus 19:18-21, 20:18-21].

The people wanted God's blessings but did not want to know God. They did not want to be intimate with the One Who not only had delivered them but also called them to give up their pettiness and selfishness and live wholeheartedly in His presence. The difference between Moses and the children of Israel is summed up in Psalm 103:7: "He made known His ways unto Moses, His doings unto the children of Israel."

How tragic! The people focused on the fire and the smoke and forgot that this terrifying, majestic God loved them [even with all their failings] and had fought for them. Since Israel rejected intimacy with God, God gave Moses the Law for Israel to follow. In providing the written Law to the people of Israel, Moses gave a forthtelling word to the people. His writings clearly defined how the people were to honor the Lord; their obedience [not love] would be the foundation of their relationship to the Lord. [Note that the Law, taken as a whole, was a forthtelling word that revealed God's righteousness and holiness]. However, Israel would discover that long-term obedience apart from love would not be possible.

While the children of Israel pulled back in fear, content to have Moses relay God's words to them, Moses yearned to know more about God. This difference was clearly defined by Israel's worship of the golden calf. Although God did not destroy the entire camp, Moses removed his tent from the center of the people and pitched his tent, along with the Tent of Meeting, on the outskirts of the camp. While Israel mourned their sin, Moses continued to commune with God and sought to know Him better. In Exodus 33:13, Moses asked God to show him His way; in Exodus 33:18, Moses asked to see God's glory.

While God did not grant Moses' request to see His full glory, He did allow Moses to see His back, and He gave Moses revelation and understanding beyond anyone else of his generation. Moses also became known as the friend of God [Exodus 33:11]. Moses grew so close to God that he began to glow with the glory of God. Moses even started wearing a veil to hide that glory from the children of Israel, who feared God's glory [Exodus 34:29-33].

Intimacy Leads to Revelation

The close communion and love between Moses and God enabled Moses to write the Pentateuch and build the Tabernacle. In the later chapters of Exodus, the text tells us repeatedly that "...*Moses did according to all that the LORD commanded him....*" Six times, this phrase appears in chapter 39 alone! Like Jesus, who knew the Father intimately and followed His will and way [John 5:19-20], Moses also followed God's will and way and built the Tabernacle according to the heavenly pattern [Hebrews 8:5; Exodus 25:40].

Even after this first generation (the generation that came out of Egypt) passed away, Moses reinstituted the Law for a new generation [Deuteronomy 5:20-24]. Once again, most Israelites chose to obey God for His blessings and not to know God intimately. Through both generations, God heard their verbal

words of affirmation, but He also saw the true motivations deep within each person's heart. Moses reminded the children of those who had perished in the wilderness that

> *And Jehovah heard the voice of your words, when ye spake unto me; and Jehovah said unto me, I have heard the voice of the words of this people, which they have spoken unto thee: they have well said all that they have spoken.* ²⁹*<u>Oh that there were such a heart in them, that they would fear me, and keep all my commandments always, that it might be well with them, and with their children forever!</u> [Deuteronomy 5:28-29. Emphasis mine]*

Yahweh and Moses knew that intimacy depends on love, not fear, and faithful obedience is based on love, not on following rules and regulations. In choosing Law over love, the people limited their blessings and wrecked their futures. Even as the people were receiving the Law, God knew they would be unable to keep it and would face harsh consequences. [Moses would sing a prophetic song warning of the destruction that Israel would endure because of disobedience (Deuteronomy 23:1-47) shortly before his death].

The tendency of Israel[5] to draw away from God defines the history of Israel. The people prove to be stubborn and rebellious. Throughout the nation's history, until the destruction that followed the second revolt against Rome, times of renewal were often followed by periods of indifference and rebellion against God. Nonetheless, throughout the Old Testament, chosen men and women passionate about their relationship with the Lord God stood before the nation as God's voice, calling the people to repent and form a relationship with God. As the Lawgiver, Moses was the first of these prophets to minister to Israel [the nation later split into the separate nations of Israel and Judah]. God never stopped yearning for His people to turn their hearts to

Him. Through the various prophets, God continually spoke to His people, warning them of the dangers of their folly and foretelling the destruction and the exile that disobedience would bring. Still, God never stopped loving His people despite their disobedience. He yearned and still yearns to have intimate fellowship with people [Ephesians 3:17].

Endnotes Chapter V: The Theocracy of Israel

[1] The people believed the lack of a king was the source of their problems, when their problems were the result of a lack of obedience to their covenant with God. However, covenant breaking brings curses no matter who the leader is.

[2] The rabbis excuse David, saying he was unaware of this requirement.

[3] Of course, the Old Testament demonstrates that all men fail to walk in perfect, complete obedience. Only Jesus was and is without sin. By faith, we stand in His righteousness. Then and now God expects us to walk in obedience to all the truth we know, trusting in His mercy and grace, to cover our failure to reach His standards. However, to know and not do is deliberate sin.

[4] While all the Israelites were originally called to serve as priests and prophets before God, worshipping the Golden Calf disqualified most of the nation.

[5] And all of humanity!

CHAPTER VI

MOSES—DELIVERER, LAWGIVER, TEACHER

We have just discussed how Moses' greatness as a leader and prophet was based on his passion for God. Moses spoke for God, conveying God's will to Pharaoh and God's love to the people of God, the children of Israel. Moses revealed God's desire to bless His people, and when the people rejected a personal relationship with God, Moses stood as their intercessor before the Lord.[1]

Moses gave Israel "the Law," the five books known as "the Pentateuch" or "the Torah." These books include Genesis, Exodus, Leviticus, Numbers, and Deuteronomy. By studying these five books, we discover the answers to many of the questions about the development of prophetic ministry in the Old Testament. Moses also answered specific questions about prophecy and prophetic ministry that still concern us today. So, let's look at some of the questions about prophetic ministry that Moses addressed:

- Can a woman be a prophetess? Yes! In Exodus 15:20, Moses writes that his sister Miriam is a prophetess.
- Can a follower of God aspire to be a prophet? Is it appropriate to want to prophesy? Yes. In Numbers 11:25-26, the Lord took some of the Spirit that rested upon Moses and gave it to seventy elders,

and it came to pass, that, when the Spirit rested upon them, they prophesied, but they did so no longer" [Numbers 11:26].

When Joshua learned these two men in the camp were prophesying, he wanted Moses to stop them. However, Moses, who knew the heart of God better than anyone else, declared,

And Moses said unto him, Art thou jealous for my sake? Would that all Jehovah's people were prophets, that Jehovah would put his Spirit upon them!" [Numbers11: 29]

Later, in the New Testament, Paul would confirm this truth [1 Corinthians 14:1, 3-5].[2]

• Could there be more than one prophet ministering simultaneously in the Old Testament? Yes. While Moses was the leader of Israel, Miriam was a prophetess, as previously stated. Later, in 1 Kings, Micaiah served as a prophet of the Lord during the same time as Elijah. References to "a company of prophets" are mentioned in the books of Samuel and Kings.

The Lord desires everyone to be a prophet, able to hear His voice and speak forth His Words [as we have seen above in Numbers 11:25-26]. By studying the later books of the Old Testament, biblical scholars have determined that the ministries of the various classical Old Testament prophets overlapped.

Notice the estimated chronology of the following Old Testament prophets:

Hosea	760-710 BC	Amos	760-750 BC
Isaiah	740-685 BC	Micah	740-690 BC

Jeremiah/Baruch 625-580 BC	Ezekiel 595-570 BC
	Zephaniah 640-610 BC
	Nahum 660-615 BC
Jeremiah/Baruch 625-580 BC	Daniel* 605-570 BC
Haggai 520 BC	Zechariah 520 BC

[The Jews classify the book of Daniel as a "writing" because Daniel did not share his revelations when he received them but wrote them down for the future.]

- If the Old Testament prophet or prophetess made a prophetic mistake, would he or she be automatically killed? No. My answer to this question may come as a surprise to you. While the simple answer to the question is no, the full answer is a bit complicated. Today, some teach that if an Old Testament prophet made any mistake in his prophesying, or if the prophecy did not come to pass, he or she was killed. However, this teaching oversimplifies what the Lord taught His people through Moses. Let's look at some examples from Scripture:
  o Moses, Miriam, and Aaron seemed to develop some sibling rivalry.

And Miriam and Aaron spake against Moses.... ⁴And Jehovah spake suddenly unto Moses, and unto Aaron, and unto Miriam.... ⁶And he said, Hear now my words: if there be a prophet among you, I Jehovah will make myself known unto him in a vision, I will speak with him in a dream. ⁷My servant Moses is not so; he is faithful in all my house: ⁸with him will I speak mouth to mouth, even manifestly, and not in dark speeches; and the form of Jehovah shall he behold: wherefore then were ye not afraid to speak against my servant, against Moses? ...¹⁰And the cloud removed from over the Tent; and, behold, Miriam was leprous, as [white as] snow: and Aaron

72

looked upon Miriam, and, behold, she was leprous....
¹³And Moses cried unto Jehovah, saying, Heal her, O
God, I beseech thee. ¹⁴And Jehovah said unto Moses,
If her father had but spit in her face, should she not be
ashamed seven days? let her be shut up without the
camp seven days, and after that she shall be brought
in again. ¹⁵And Miriam was shut up without the
camp seven days: and the people journeyed not till
Miriam was brought in again [Numbers 12:1-14].

This passage recounts an instance when Miriam and
Aaron spoke out against Moses. We have already
ascertained that Miriam was a prophetess [and Aaron
was the high priest]. Therefore, Miriam's words carried
great weight with the children of Israel, for when she
spoke, the people assumed she spoke God's words.
However, though the Lord was displeased with her
critical attitude and struck her with leprosy, she was
not killed, even though her words "angered the Lord"
[v.9].

o Let's look at another example of a prophet speaking
incorrectly. This incident occurred during the time
of King David. The Scripture we want to examine is
found in 2 Samuel 7. In this chapter, when David told
the prophet Nathan that he wished to build a temple
for God, Nathan replied, *"Go! Do all that is in your
heart, for the LORD is with you"* [v.3]. While Nathan
invoked the authority of God in his reply to David,
God corrected Nathan that night [v. 4]. However,
God did not condemn Nathan; instead, he merely
corrected him. God revealed that His plan and way
were far more significant than either David or Nathan
had considered, for the Messiah would come through
David's family.

*Now therefore tell my servant David this, 'Yahweh
of Armies says, "I took you from the sheep pen, from*

following the sheep, to be prince over my people, over Israel.... ¹²When your days are fulfilled, and you sleep with your fathers, I will set up your offspring after you, who will proceed out of your body, and I will establish his kingdom. ¹³He will build a house for my name, and I will establish the throne of his kingdom forever. ¹⁴I will be his father, and he will be my son. If he commits iniquity, I will chasten him with the rod of men, and with the stripes of the children of men; ¹⁵but my loving kindness will not depart from him, as I took it from Saul, whom I put away before you. ¹⁶Your house and your kingdom will be made sure forever before you. Your throne will be established forever." [2 Samuel 7:8, 12-16, WEB]

o The book of Jonah provides our well-known third example. God told Jonah to go to the city of Nineveh and proclaim that the city would be destroyed. However, once the reluctant prophet finally obeyed God and prophesied over the city, the city repented, and God appeared to change His mind. Nineveh was not destroyed, causing Jonah to sulk [Jonah 3-4]. God had spoken judgment over Nineveh through Jonah. However, when the city repented, God chose not to destroy the city. Jonah's prophecy was not fulfilled as he had declared, but this did not make him a false prophet deserving of death.³

o Our fourth example is the most extreme. You can read the entire story in 1 Kings chapter 13. Let me summarize: In 1 Kings 13:1-10, the account states that an unnamed prophet was sent from Judah to confront Jeroboam, the king of Israel [Israel had become a separate kingdom distinct from the kingdom of Judah]. The king got angry and tried to hit the prophet, but the king's hand instantly withered. The prophet restored the king's hand, and the king offered him hospitality. The prophet refused his hospitality, explaining in verse nine:

for so was it charged me by the word of Jehovah,
saying, Thou shalt eat no bread, nor drink water,
neither return by the way that thou camest [1 Kings
13:9].

The prophet then left the king. However, the young prophet ran into an old prophet living in Beit-El during his journey home. The old prophet had heard of the young prophet's encounter with the king and invited the young prophet to his home for dinner. The older man was so anxious to talk to the young man that he lied to the young prophet. The older man said,

And he said unto him, I also am a prophet as thou art;
and an angel spake unto me by the word of Jehovah,
saying, Bring him back with thee into thy house, that
he may eat bread and drink water. [But] he lied unto
him [1 Kings 13:18].

The young prophet believed the older man, so he accompanied him home and ate dinner with him. However, because he disobeyed the original instructions from the Lord, the young prophet was killed on the way home. Yet the Scripture records no punishment for the older prophet, even though he deliberately lied!

So, what does the Scripture say about a prophet's responsibilities? Let's look at Deuteronomy 13:1-6:

If a prophet or a dreamer of dreams arises among
you, and he gives you a sign or a wonder, ²and the
sign or the wonder comes to pass, of which he spoke
to you, saying, "Let's go after other gods" (which
you have not known) "and let's serve them," ³you
shall not listen to the words of that prophet, or to

that dreamer of dreams; for Yahweh your God is testing you, to know whether you love Yahweh your God with all your heart and with all your soul. ⁴You shall walk after Yahweh your God, fear him, keep his commandments, and obey his voice. You shall serve him, and cling to him. ⁵That prophet, or that dreamer of dreams, shall be put to death, because he has spoken rebellion against Yahweh your God, who brought you out of the land of Egypt and redeemed you out of the house of bondage, to draw you aside out of the way which Yahweh your God commanded you to walk in. So you shall remove the evil from among you.

If your brother, the son of your mother, or your son, or your daughter, or the wife of your bosom, or your friend who is as your own soul, entices you secretly, saying, "Let's go and serve other gods"—which you have not known, you, nor your fathers; ⁷of the gods of the peoples who are around you, near to you, or far off from you, from the one end of the earth even to the other end of the earth— ⁸you shall not consent to him nor listen to him; neither shall your eye pity him, neither shall you spare, neither shall you conceal him; ⁹but you shall surely kill him. . . . [Deuteronomy 13:1-9, WEB].

Take a moment to read over this again. Please notice what Moses said in verse five:

That prophet, or that dreamer of dreams, shall be put to death, <u>because he has spoken rebellion against Yahweh your God,</u> [some translations say, "he has spoken to turn you away from"] against Jehovah your God . . . , to draw you aside [or "to thrust you out" or "to make you leave"] which Jehovah thy God commanded you to walk in [Deuteronomy 13:5, WEB. Emphasis mine. Additional comments mine].

In this passage of Scripture, Moses states that if a prophet or other person sought to lead Israel away from God, he or she should be executed. Moses reiterates the importance of loyalty and obedience to God in verses seven through twelve. Moses declared loyalty to God the Father, and His commandments overrode even the closest family ties. Moses even extended the death sentence to entire cities if they drew away from the Lord [Deuteronomy 13:12-18].

Moses made it clear: Whether the speaker was a prophet, a beloved family member, an honored elder, or a city's inhabitants, if they sought to lead Israel away from God, they were to be destroyed. <u>The plum line of evaluation was this: Did the prophet's words turn the people's hearts away from God?</u> How the prophet's words impacted the people's attitude toward God was the key, not whether they made a mistake or an inaccurate statement.

Moses also spoke about prophets in Deuteronomy 18. In chapter 18, verses 9-22, Moses again teaches the difference between true prophets and the false prophets who spoke presumptuously, practicing divination and consulting demonic spirits.

> "When thou art come into the land ..., thou shalt not learn to do after the abominations of those nations. [10]There shall not be found with thee any one that maketh his son or his daughter to pass through the fire, one that useth divination, one that practiseth augury, or an enchanter, or a sorcerer, [11]or a charmer, or a consulter with a familiar spirit, or a wizard, or a necromancer. [12]For whosoever doeth these things is an abomination unto Jehovah: [Deuteronomy 18:9-12].

All soothsayers, enchanters, sorcerers, charmers, divinators, wizards, or necromancers, as mentioned in Deuteronomy 18, were abominations to God and were to be driven out [or killed]. Israel was never to have dealings with any of them[4]. [King Saul did so and was sentenced to death by God as God's judgment on his disobedience—1 Samuel 28:1-20]. In contrast to these false guides, God would establish true prophets for the people to listen to. [Notice that verses 18-19 are a prophetic description of the Lord Jesus Himself.]

> *I will raise them up a prophet from among their brethren, like unto thee; and I will put my words in his mouth, and he shall speak unto them all that I shall command him. [19]And it shall come to pass, that whosoever will not hearken unto my words which he shall speak in my name, I will require it of him [Deuteronomy 18:18-19].*

Moses then concluded the chapter by providing guidance for determining whether a prophet was false or should be respected, feared, and listened to.

> *But the prophet, that shall speak a word presumptuously in my name, which I have not commanded him to speak, or that shall speak in the name of other gods, that same prophet shall die. [21]And if thou say in thy heart, How shall we know the word which Jehovah hath not spoken? [22]when a prophet speaketh in the name of Jehovah, if the thing follow not, nor come to pass, that is the thing which Jehovah hath not spoken: the prophet hath spoken it presumptuously, thou shalt not be afraid of him [Deuteronomy 18:20-22. Emphasis mine].*

On the surface, Deuteronomy 18:20-22 judges anyone who makes any mistake or error in prophesying. It seems to condemn to death anyone whose prophecy fails to come true

or fails to come to pass. However, let us examine Jonah's prophecy about the destruction of Nineveh; this prophecy did not come true, as the city was not destroyed within forty days. The people repented, and God withdrew His wrath. Jonah was not condemned as a false prophet, although God did reprove his unforgiving attitude toward the people of the city.

How do we reconcile the story of Jonah with Moses' teaching? Look at Deuteronomy 18:20 more closely. As you do, remember what kind of person Moses was speaking of in these verses. Moses was not speaking about anyone who mentioned an idea or suggested violating the Torah in a minor way. Look at verse 20 first:

> ²⁰*But the prophet, that shall speak a word presumptuously in my name, which I have not commanded him to speak, or that shall speak in the name of other gods, that same prophet shall die [Deuteronomy 18:20. Emphasis mine].*

Notice that the second part of the verse ["that same prophet shall die"] echoes what Moses wrote in Deuteronomy 13. The prophet who attempted to lead Israel into worshipping any god other than Yahweh was to be killed. The prophet who represented himself as a follower or representative of a different God from Yahweh was Yahweh's enemy—and by extension—an enemy of Israel. Such an enemy was to be removed.

What about the first part of verse 20? Let's read this:

> *But the prophet, that shall speak a word presumptuously in my name.... [Deuteronomy 18:20, part a. Emphasis mine].*

The precise meaning of this portion of Deuteronomy 18:20 pivots upon two words. The first word is "prophet". Remember the definition of an Old Testament prophet. In the Old Testament, a prophet was a person selected by God to be His representative. God had chosen this person to fellowship with Him, to receive a glimpse of God's heart, and to act as God's envoy. This was the man or woman whom God sent the Holy Spirit to rest upon.

As the prophet of God functioning in the Theocracy and later during the Kingdom age, the prophet or prophetess had the privilege and responsibility to represent God's will to the people so that they might please God, receive His blessings, and avoid the curses of disobedience. For one called and appointed, to speak against the Lord or twist His will was the deepest betrayal of a sacred trust. Such a person had become a reflection of Satan, the created being who rebelled against the Elohim, forsaking the goodness and greatness of the Lord out of a lust for glory[5].

Now, let's look at the rest of Deuteronomy 18:20a. The second word that this section [section "a"] pivots upon is the word "presumptuously" [or "presume" in some translations]. This is the Hebrew word YAZIDH, which means "to be presumptuous." Typically, this word refers to "proud behavior," characterized by acting insolently against God or in a proud and rebellious manner. In other words, Moses is telling the people of Israel that a person who deliberately speaks against the Lord, while exhibiting a self-serving, proud, and rebellious attitude, is not to be feared, shown respect, or listened to. Such a person is trying to lead the people away from God and is to be put to death.[6] He is not speaking of someone who makes a mistake, as Nathan did. Miriam's attitude came close to this, so God Himself corrected her prideful, spiteful boldness. He did not kill her; He showed her mercy. Jonah's prophecy of destruction for the city of Nineveh was conditional. The prophecy's lack of

fulfillment reflected God's heart's desire for the people to heed the prophetic word and repent.

This understanding puts a different spin on Moses' statement, doesn't it?

After David and Solomon died, the Kingdom split into Judah and the northern kingdom of Israel. During King Ahab's reign in Israel, the prophets of Baal deliberately led the people away from God to worship Baal. Thus, when Elijah defeated the prophets of Baal on Mt. Carmel by proving Yahweh was the true God, Elijah executed the prophets of Baal as the Law commanded [1 Kings 18:40].

God did not condemn people for honest mistakes. He condemned those who deliberately misled the people or prophesied for personal reward [see Ezekiel 34, Jeremiah 2:8, 5:9-14; 1 Kings 22:10-11, 24]. He also judged the kings and people who listened to these false prophets and ignored His true prophets and the Law [See Jeremiah 23:11-37].

Endnotes Chapter VI: Moses—Deliverer, Lawgiver, Teacher

[1]Exodus 32 demonstrates the lengths Moses would go in his work of intercession for Israel. He was willing to die on behalf of a people who seemed unable to understand the reality of Yahweh and His desire to bless them.
[2]However, there are responsibilities as well as blessings for the prophet. These responsibilities must be understood. The Bible warns against selfish or frivolous ministry that leads others astray. [See Romans 2:17-23, Acts 20:28–31; 1 Timothy 6:3–6; and Matthew 18:6-7].
[3]Nineveh was destroyed later when she returned to her evil ways.

[4]God did want Israel to walk in the supernatural but only with Him! God was to be the source of their revelation and power.

[5]Satan once stood in the very presence of God:

> [14]*Thou wast the anointed cherub that covereth: and I set thee, so that thou wast upon the holy mountain of God; thou hast walked up and down in the midst of the stones of fire [Ezekiel. 28:14].*

[6]David C. Grabbe has written an excellent discussion on false prophets in <u>Forerunner</u>, "Prophecy Watch," Sept.-Oct. 2006. This can be found at: www.cgg.org/index.cfm/fuseaction/Library.sr/CT/PW/k/1177/False-Prophet.htm. Other articles include: "How to Detect a Charlatan and a False Prophet" 2 catholicshare.com/how-to-detect-a-charlatan-and-a-false-prophet/. Accessed November 2025. https:fr.bilsorthodoxblog.com/203/12/01-prophets-true-and-false-old-and-new-part 1/ [and there is also a part 2!]. Accessed November 2025.

CHAPTER VII

THE THEOCRACY AFTER MOSES

Joshua: Showing Courage for God

The events surrounding King Ahab, Elijah, and Jeremiah happened hundreds of years after Moses led the Hebrews out of Egypt. Much occurred in Israel's Theocracy during those years.

After the death of Moses, Joshua became the leader of Israel. Joshua knew the ways of the Lord, for Joshua had the heart to know God. Even as a young man, he was Moses' helper [Exodus 24:12-18] and often lingered at the tent of meeting [Exodus 33:11]. God spoke to Joshua [Joshua 1:5-9, 5:2] and gave Joshua instructions for Israel [Joshua 1:10-11, 16-18; 5:4-7].

In Joshua 1, the Lord spoke to Joshua and declared:

> *Only be strong and very courageous, to observe to do according to all the law, which Moses my servant commanded thee: turn not from it to the right hand or to the left, that thou mayest have good success whithersoever thou goest. ⁸This book of the law shall not depart out of thy mouth, but thou shalt meditate thereon day and night, that thou mayest observe to do according to all that is written therein: for then thou*

shalt make thy way prosperous, and then thou shalt have good success. ⁹Have not I commanded thee? Be strong and of good courage; be not affrighted, neither be thou dismayed: for Jehovah thy God is with thee whithersoever thou goes [Joshua 1:7-9].

In Joshua 24, Joshua prophesied to the people, speaking a forthtelling word from God:

And Joshua said unto all the people, Thus saith Jehovah, the God of Israel, Your fathers dwelt of old time beyond the River, even Terah, the father of Abraham, and the father of Nahor: and they served other gods. ³And I took your father Abraham from beyond the River, and led him throughout all the land of Canaan, and multiplied his seed, and gave him Isaac....

⁵And I sent Moses and Aaron, and I plagued Egypt, according to that which I did in the midst thereof: and afterward I brought you out. ⁶And I brought your fathers out of Egypt: and ye came unto the sea; and the Egyptians pursued after your fathers with chariots and with horsemen unto the Red Sea. ⁷And when they cried out unto Jehovah, he put darkness between you and the Egyptians, and brought the sea upon them, and covered them; and your eyes saw what I did in Egypt: and ye dwelt in the wilderness many days.

⁸And I brought you into the land of the Amorites, ...; and I gave them into your hand, and ye possessed their land; and I destroyed them from before you. ⁹Then Balak the son of Zippor, king of Moab, arose and fought against Israel: and he sent and called Balaam the son of Beor to curse you; ¹⁰but I would not hearken unto Balaam; therefore he blessed you still: .... ¹¹And ye went over the Jordan, and came unto Jericho: and the men of Jericho fought against you,

the Amorite, and the Perizzite, and the Canaanite, and the Hittite, and the Girgashite, the Hivite, and the Jebusite; and I delivered them into your hand.

¹²And I sent the hornet before you, which drove them out from before you, even the two kings of the Amorites; not with thy sword, nor with thy bow. ¹³And I gave you a land whereon thou hadst not labored, and cities which ye built not, and ye dwell therein; of vineyards and olive yards which ye planted not do ye eat.

¹⁴Now therefore fear Jehovah, and serve him in sincerity and in truth; and put away the gods which your fathers served beyond the River, and in Egypt; and serve ye Jehovah.

¹⁵And if it seem evil unto you to serve Jehovah, choose you this day whom ye will serve; whether the gods which your fathers served that were beyond the River, or the gods of the Amorites, in whose land ye dwell: but as for me and my house, we will serve Jehovah [Joshua 24: 2-3, 5-15].

God also demonstrated His support for Joshua's being His chosen messenger through miracles. God parted the Jordan [Joshua 4:8-24] and pulled down the walls of Jericho [Joshua 6] as the people obeyed the commands that God relayed through Joshua.

However, while the book of Joshua records Joshua's receiving his battle strategies from God, the terms "prophet" or "prophecy" never appear. Nevertheless, Joshua is recognized as one of the early or "former" prophets because Joshua had a heart for God and spoke God's words to Israel. God also made the sun stand still at Joshua's request [Joshua 10:12]. Joshua repeated God's directions for attacking Jericho and other cities [Joshua 5:13; 6:19] and exhorted the people to remain faithful to the covenant [Joshua 24:15-27].

The Time of the Judges

After Joshua died, Israel no longer had a national leader; the tribes were self-governing, except when leaders arose who were called "Judges." As I mentioned earlier, during the Judges' time, a cycle of obedience, apathy, disobedience, persecution, and repentance developed from Israel's failure to maintain a continual, loving, and obedient relationship with God. The primary focus of a judge during this period was often on arbitrating disagreements among the people, not to speak for God. However, when a crisis arose, leading the disobedient and apathetic Israelites to repent, God would raise up a judge to deliver the people from their enemies. Sometimes, a prophet appeared. However, while more than twelve judges are named in the Bible, only a few of those listed in Judges are known to have personally encountered the Lord. These people were

- Deborah—Deborah prophesied the victory of Barak over Sisera [Judges 4:1-5:31].
- "A prophet"—reproved the Israelites for not listening to the Lord and following Him [Judges 6:7-10].
- Gideon [Jerub-Baal, son of Joash]—When the angel of the Lord called him the champion of Israel, Gideon responded in faith and led the people of Manasseh into a great victory over the Midianites [Judges 6:1-8:32; Hebrews. 11:32].
- Phinehas, son of Eleazar—Phinehas inquired of the Lord for Israel and received direction from the Lord for the children of Israel to attack Benjamin [Judges 20:28].

Of all these people, only Deborah and the unnamed prophet of Judges 6:7-10 seem to demonstrate a solid prophetic gifting, speaking for God with the authority of the Lord. They alone are named "prophets". As stated in 1 Samuel 3:1b, *"And the word of Jehovah was precious in those days; there was no frequent vision."*

Why was the prophetic voice so lacking during the time of the judges, a time of cyclical failure for Israel, when one might expect the people would be hungry to hear the voice of the Lord? Had God grown tired of speaking to Israel because of their continual disobedience? No. The truth was that few people were willing to hear and to follow God's voice closely. God was speaking, but few were willing to serve as His messenger. The issue was not one of need. The issue was the lethargy of the people of whom few were willing to be intimate with the Lord.

The Danger of Apathy

The Book of Judges demonstrates that although Israel was called to be God's special people, the majority did not embrace or desire a special relationship with God. <u>They wanted blessing without relationship.</u> They sought to obtain what required a heartfelt commitment to a covenant relationship through outward obedience.

Obedience to God's Law was often treated as a matter of convenience. A *laissez-faire* attitude toward God infected the entire population. Even Samson, ordained as God's servant before his birth, was casual in observing the Law and honoring God with his life [although he repented before his death — Judges 13-16].

The Last Prophet of the Theocracy

Samuel, the last of the great judges, served God from his miraculous birth until his death. He became God's divinely commissioned messenger and served in several important positions during his life, earning God's favor <u>because he knew how to obey.</u> Samuel's story began when his then-barren mother, Hannah, prayed to God for a child. She became pregnant and named her baby "Samuel," which means "the

Lord hears" or "heard by the Lord" [See 1 Samuel 1:20]. After the boy was weaned, Hannah presented him to God at Shiloh, placing Samuel in the care of Eli, the high priest. Samuel did not initially recognize the voice of the Lord [1 Samuel 3:4-15]. Nevertheless, Samuel grew in wisdom and became a prophet recognized by the people [1 Samuel 3:20] as God's spokesman.

Although Samuel was primarily called a prophet, he became the functioning leader and judge over all of Israel after Eli the High Priest died following a great Philistine victory over the Israelites [1 Samuel 4]. Once the ark was returned, Samuel rallied the nation against the Philistines at Mizpah. Samuel became the leader of Israel, functioning much as Moses once had. Samuel established his home in Ramah and traveled in a circuit throughout Israel to settle the people's disputes.

Before Samuel's time, a prophet was referred to as a "seer." [1 Samuel 9:9]. But Samuel was not just a forecaster of the future but became a "mouthpiece" for God. He delivered God's words to individuals and Israel. God first called him to inform Eli that his house [that is, his entire family] would be punished for the abuses and perversions his sons committed in their role as priests. [The priest was to be a mediator for God to the people and for the people to God, but Eli's sons made a mockery of the priesthood—1 Samuel 3:11-18]. Samuel also rebuked the nation for their evil ways and called the people to repent [1 Samuel 7:3].

However, Samuel was not perfect. In his later life, Samuel overstepped his authority as a judge. Samuel appointed his sons as judges over Israel without any directive from God to do so. Samuel's sons, Joel and Abijah, were corrupt, so the people demanded a king [1 Samuel 8:1-5][1]. After praying about this problem, Samuel listened to God and anointed Saul, a tall, handsome man, as the first king of Israel [1 Samuel 10:17-26]. Later, in his farewell speech to Israel, Samuel warned the people to serve the true God. He said if King Saul disobeyed the Lord, God would sweep them away [1 Samuel 12:1-15].

Although Samuel released his role as judge and leader to Saul, Samuel continued to function as the Lord's prophet. Unfortunately, King Saul did disobey God [1 Samuel 13:9-13; 1 Samuel 15:1-23]. Samuel, the former leader, had to confront Saul and speak God's prophetic judgment over him [1 Samuel 15:26-29]. God would later direct Samuel to prophetically anoint David as king over Israel [1 Samuel 16:1-13]. Thus, in His last years, Samuel foreshadowed the later prophets' role in establishing and admonishing the kings of Israel and Judah.

School of the Prophet

Samuel may also have established the "school of the prophets" during this period. The Bible does not state that Samuel established the school; the Bible does mention that such schools existed during the time of Elijah and Elisha [1 Kings 20:35; 2 Kings 2:3, 5, 15]. The precise role or importance of these schools in relation to the named prophets of the Bible is unknown. While the Old Testament names various prophets, none is described as a "graduate" of a prophetic school.

The Biblical accounts reveal that not all prophets went to a formal school for training. Elisha, for example, became Elijah's servant and apprentice, and Amos was a herdsman from Tekoa [Amos 1:1] until the Lord called him to prophesy to the northern kingdom of Israel.

If the influence of these prophetic schools is so ambiguous, how can we understand why they were established? While a definitive answer is impossible, the book of 1 Samuel may offer some insight.

The Bible demonstrates that God is a God of order [1 Corinthians 14:33, 40]. However, during the time of Samuel, prophetic ministry often appeared to be without order, involving public, ecstatic displays. An account of such a

display appears in 1 Samuel 19:18-24, in which the power of God falls on Saul and causes him to strip his robes off![2]

> *Now David fled, and escaped, and came to Samuel to Ramah,...* [23]*And he [Saul—my insert] went thither to Naioth in Ramah: and the Spirit of God came upon him also, and he went on, and prophesied, until he came to Naioth in Ramah.* [24]*And he also stripped off his clothes, and he also prophesied before Samuel, and lay down naked all that day and all that night. Wherefore they say, Is Saul also among the prophets?*
> *[1 Samuel 19:18-24]*

Prophetic ministry is not dry; emotions are involved. However, similar ecstatic displays were a well-known trait of pagan religious ceremonies and diviners. Pagan religions often used emotions and drugs to produce a sense of euphoria, trances, and altered mental states. [The prophets of Baal, who opposed Elijah on Mt. Carmel, attempted to enter a frenzied state to get Baal to react—1 Kings 18:22-29].

While ecstatic displays were and are part of the prophetic tradition, <u>the core of faithful prophetic ministry lies in the intimate relationship between the prophet and the Lord God.</u> Young prophets needed [and still need] to learn how to put aside their problems or desires to focus on knowing God ultimately and discovering on the message that God wished to convey. The schools of the prophets may have been created to nurture those called into prophetic ministry. These schools may have sought to help young prophets by

- teaching them the importance of focusing on their relationship with God,
- training them to maintain integrity in their walk before men,
- and teaching them how to confront governmental leaders in a respectful yet powerful manner.

Transition Under the Kings

Samuel was the first prophet to stand before a king as the voice of the Lord. Although Samuel had functioned in a Moses-like position of prophet and judge, Samuel was forced out of his Theocratic leadership position when the people demanded a king. After Saul was crowned king, Samuel acted as Saul's advisor [1 Samuel 15:1-3] and as the voice of the Lord to the king. While providing Saul direction, Samuel also reproved Saul [1 Samuel 15:17-27] for not fully obeying the Lord. Later, Samuel also acted as God's agent to anoint David. As the first prophet standing in the role of the King's advisor, Samuel gained great wisdom that he could pass on to other prophets.

It was important for a prophet to understand how to conduct oneself before the king. As stated, once the monarchy was established, the role of the prophet underwent a change. The prophet became an advisor and the king's conscience instead of being the leader himself [as Moses and Samuel both were]. While kings often sought the prophet's advice, they were not always happy to receive it. During the reign of David, Nathan the prophet advised David about David's desire to build God a temple [2 Samuel 7:1-3]. Nathan revealed the Lord's will for David's son to build the temple and foretold the coming of Jesus [2 Samuel 7:4-17]. Later, the same Nathan confronted David about his adultery with Bathsheba and the murder of Uriah [2 Samuel 12]. At the end of David's life, Nathan revealed God's will for Solomon to be anointed king in David's old age [1 Kings 1-2].

However, the cordial relationship between David and Nathan did not extend to other kings and the various prophets who functioned during their reigns. While the various kings of Israel and Judah often sought the public approval of the prophets [and of Yahweh], they greatly resented the Lord's correction through His prophets. Even Nathan had carefully framed his

confrontation with David over his sin with Bathsheba with a story. Nathan's wisdom, inspired by God, enabled him to penetrate the king's mental and emotional defenses, thereby preserving his own life and liberty. He cleverly told a pitiful story of a lamb to awaken David's sense of justice, only to declare at the end, "Thou art the man" [2 Samuel 12:7].

In the later years of the divided kingdoms, prophets continued to act as the king's conscience. King Jeroboam 1 of Israel tried to strike the prophet who corrected him [1 Kings 13:1-11], although a prophet had previously anointed him as King [1 Kings 26-39]. 1 Kings 22:1-28 and 2 Chronicles 18:1-19:1 speak of the friction between the prophet Micaiah and King Ahab. Ahab ignored Micaiah's prophetic warning and died in battle [1 Kings 22:15- 18, 37]. These incidents reveal the prophet's challenge in maintaining a close, intimate relationship with the Lord and speaking God's truth boldly, even when his prophecies were unpopular. While the children of Israel had occasionally challenged Moses' leadership and had even threatened to stone him during the time of the Theocracy, more than one prophet was imprisoned or executed by his king.

Summary and Conclusion

The prophet's life was neither glamorous nor always enjoyable. We have seen that the role of the prophet was a ministry that required dedication to listening to God's voice and proclaiming His words. Moses, the first prophet of the Theocracy, was considered the greatest of all the prophets of Israel. Although Moses originally entered his call half-heartedly and reluctantly, God captured his heart. Moses was faithful in delivering God's Words to those who rejected the opportunity to know God intimately.

Prophetic voices continued to speak for God during the time of the judges. The last judge, Samuel, was the most

outstanding judge and the most influential prophet since Moses. However, the people wanted a king, and the prophetic role changed from that of a leader to being an advisor once the kingdom was established under Saul. Throughout the kingdom age of Israel, the kings and people who listened to prophetic counsels prospered, and those who ignored them did so at their own personal peril.

Endnotes Chapter VII: The Theocracy after Moses

[1] Samuel did not cause Israel to sin. However, his poor judgment concerning his sons opened the door for the people to express their discontent. Samuel's sons became the excuse and justification for demanding a king "like the other nations." See 1 Samuel 8.

[2] We will return to this passage to discuss the spiritual aspects of this event later.

[3] For example, Jewish tradition states Manasseh killed Isaiah by having him "sawn asunder" [see Hebrews 11:34]. King Joash had Zechariah stoned [2 Chronicles 24:20-22; Hebrews 11:37]. King Zedekiah had Jeremiah imprisoned [Jeremiah 37: 13-21].

CHAPTER VIII

THE LATTER, CLASSICAL OLD TESTAMENT PROPHETS

In the last chapter, we saw how the role of the prophet changed when Israel transitioned from a theocracy to a kingdom. No longer directly governing the people as the regent of God, the prophet had become an advisor to the king and sometimes his challenger. When the kings of Israel [and later the kings of Israel and Judah] listened to the prophetic voices of God's servants, the kingdoms flourished. However, as the kingship became more secularized and the people's religious life became politicized,[1] the prophetic voices that God established were often ignored. The ultimate result of this trend was foreign domination and exile. However, God never ceased calling out to His people to listen to Him and heed the voices of His prophets.

Individual prophetic books emerged during this kingdom age of Israel [approximately 1050-650 BC], which included the time of the United Kingdom, the Northern Kingdom of Israel, and the Southern Kingdom of Judah. These books would be added to the Pentateuch to form the bulk of the Old Testament. The prophetic books included various teachings, warnings, calls for repentance, and encouraging words from Adonai to the Hebrew people. These books recorded and explained God's dealings with Israel and the nations surrounding her.

Most scholars believe that these classical prophetic books were written between 800 BC and 400 BC. Besides warning the people of God's judgment against disobedience, these works also contained a growing Messianic thread. Even as Israel and the latter divided kingdoms of Judah and Israel repeatedly and willfully broke their covenant with Yahweh, God spoke through His prophets of a coming "anointed one" who would restore all that was broken. Judgment loomed, but this "anointed one" would restore all things at the proper time.

When we examine the Old Testament in a modern edition of the Bible, we find that it contains six major prophetic books: Isaiah, Jeremiah, Baruch, Lamentations, Ezekiel, and Daniel. [Note: Protestants do not recognize Baruch as part of the canon.]

- The Book of Isaiah was written during the reigns of several kings of Judah. The first portion of the book was a call for the Israelite people [primarily Judah] to either repent or face judgment. The second half of the book spoke of God's forgiveness. Isaiah also contains some of the best-known passages concerning the coming of the Messiah.

  The people that walked in darkness have seen a great light: they that dwelt in the land of the shadow of death, upon them hath the light shined.... [6]For unto us a child is born, unto us a son is given; and the government shall be upon his shoulder: and his name shall be called Wonderful, Counselor, Mighty God, Everlasting Father, Prince of Peace. [7]Of the increase of his government and of peace, there shall be no end, upon the throne of David, and upon his kingdom, to establish it, and to uphold it with justice and with righteousness from henceforth even forever. The zeal of Jehovah of hosts will perform this [Isaiah 9:2, 6-7].

- The Book of Jeremiah warned that destruction was imminent if the people did not repent of their sin and social callousness. After Jerusalem was destroyed, Jeremiah declared the Messiah would come and restore Israel.

A lion is gone up from his thicket, and a destroyer of nations; he is on his way, he is gone forth from his place, to make thy land desolate, that thy cities be laid waste, without inhabitant [Jeremiah 4:7].

This book is also highly personal as Jeremiah records his emotional struggles to declare God's judgment while enduring active persecution.

⁷O Jehovah, thou hast persuaded me, and I was persuaded; thou art stronger than I, and hast prevailed: I am become a laughing-stock all the day, every one mocketh me [Jeremiah 20:7].

- Although the Book of Lamentations does not name its author, scholars agree that Jeremiah was the likely author. This poetic book provides an eyewitness account of Jerusalem's destruction but closes with the hope that a sovereign, loving God might bring restoration to His people.

Mine eyes do fail with tears, my heart is troubled; My liver is poured upon the earth, because of the destruction of the daughter of my people, Because the young children and the sucklings swoon in the streets of the city [Lamentations 2:11].

²¹This I recall to my mind; therefore have I hope. ²²[It is of] Jehovah's lovingkindnesses that we are not consumed, because his compassions fail not [Lamentations 3:21-22].

- Ezekiel's prophetic ministry overlapped that of Jeremiah's, but Ezekiel was in exile while Jeremiah lived in Jerusalem. Ezekiel predicts Jerusalem would be destroyed because she refused to repent and give up her idolatry. Ezekiel's book is known for its unique and vivid imagery. Some of the best-known images described in Ezekiel are his vision of the "wheel within the wheel" (acknowledging the transcendence and power of God [Ezekiel 1]); Ezekiel's vision of a new, glorious temple [Ezekiel 40-48]; and his vision of the valley of dry bones [Ezekiel 37:1-14].

¹The hand of Jehovah was upon me, and he brought me out in the Spirit of Jehovah, and set me down in the midst of the valley; and it was full of bones....⁴Again he said unto me, Prophesy over these bones, and say unto them, O ye dry bones, hear the word of Jehovah. ⁵Thus saith the Lord Jehovah unto these bones: Behold, I will cause breath to enter into you, and ye shall live. ⁶And I will lay sinews upon you, and will bring up flesh upon you, and cover you with skin, and put breath in you, and ye shall live; and ye shall know that I am Jehovah [Ezekiel 37:1, 4-6].

- The Book of Baruch consists of four major sections, that surround the fall of Jerusalem to the Babylonians. Although not part of the Jewish canon [which is why Protestants exclude it from their canon], the book, thought to have been written by Jeremiah's scribe, calls for repentance by the Jews and comments on the Jewish exile in Babylon.

...in the land of their captivities they shall remember themselves. And shall know that I am the Lord their God: for I will give them an heart, and ears to hear: And they shall praise me in the land of their

captivity, and think upon my name, And return from their stiff neck, and from their wicked deeds: for they shall remember the way of their fathers, which sinned before the Lord. And I will bring them again into the land which I promised with an oath unto their fathers, Abraham, Isaac, and Jacob, and they shall be lords of it: and I will increase them, and they shall not be diminished. And I will make an everlasting covenant with them to be their God, and they shall be my people: and I will no more drive my people of Israel out of the land that I have given them [Baruch 2:30-35, WEB]

- The last major prophetic book in the Christian Old Testament is the Book of Daniel.[2] This book was written during the time of Judah's exile in Babylon and the overthrow of Babylon by the Persian-Median empire. While the book's first part tells the story of Daniel and his friend's faithfulness under challenging circumstances, the second part of the book, chapters six through twelve, records a series of visions that Daniel experienced. These visions deal with the rise and fall of various empires and the trials that Israel endures before the Messiah delivers her and sets up His kingdom.

There are also twelve minor prophetic books [which are considered as one book in the Hebrew canon] included in the compilation of the Old Testament:

Hosea	Nahum
Joel	Habakkuk
Amos	Zephaniah
Obadiah	Haggai
Jonah	Zechariah
Micah	Malachi

These so-called "Minor Prophets" are referred to as "Minor" because they are relatively short. These prophetic books [or the "Book of 12"] address the sins of the nations and God's response to them. These books also contain many familiar Messianic prophecies, such as the location of Jesus' birth [see Micah 5:2].[4]

As this brief survey reveals, the Old Testament is a prophetic record containing the written words of prophets who interacted with Israel and Judah, continually calling the people to honor their covenantal relationship with Yahweh. Unfortunately, the prophets' words were often ignored or mocked until much later, when they brought comfort to a people who had been buffeted by exile and oppression.

The Impact of the Prophetic Word

Now, there were what we might consider prophetic successes during the Kingdom age that occurred when a people or a king responded to the warnings and teachings of the prophet. The people of Nineveh, confronted by Jonah after he was released from the mouth of "the great fish," heeded his warning of coming judgment and humbled themselves before God [much to Jonah's dismay]. King David listened and submitted to the words of Nathan the prophet [1 Chronicles 17:1-15] and Gad the seer [1 Chronicles 21:9-19]. King Rehoboam received a blessing when he followed the prophetic mandate to leave Jeroboam alone [2 Chronicles 11:1-23]. Later, because Rehoboam humbled himself, God delivered him from destruction during Shishak's invasion [2 Chronicles 12:1-12]. Asa prospered and was blessed when he listened to the prophet Azariah [2 Chronicles 15:8]. Jehoshaphat submitted to a prophetic rebuke and was blessed [2 Chronicles 19:1-11; 20:1-29]. Amaziah listened to the prophet and won a decisive battle [2 Chronicles 21:12-15]. Hezekiah received God's help

and blessing after seeking guidance from Isaiah [2 Chronicles 32:20].

Yet even among these successes, pride and disobedience abounded. King Rehoboam lost much of his wealth, security, and legacy because he became proud and disobedient; only his hasty repentance saved him from being destroyed by Shishak. While established through a prophetic ministry, Jeroboam's kingdom ultimately ended with the destruction of his lineage because he disobeyed God and ignored His prophetic warnings. King Asa's later disobedience eclipsed much of his early success and blessings.

Thus, as we examine the ministry of the prophets, we notice that their efforts resemble those of modern baseball players in one way: there were more apparent failures than successes. Remember: For every hit in baseball where the batter successfully connects with the ball and advances to base safely, the same batter strikes out, fouls out, or has their ball caught for an out far more often. The "batting averages" for prophets being correctly received were much worse than those of any major league baseball player! However, the prophet's stakes were consistently far higher than a baseball player's: Israel's life and the prophet's life often depended on whether the prophet got a "hit" [his words were listened to and received].

Despite their efforts to protect, warn, and encourage the people, many prophets faced persecution and even death. Nevertheless, their love for the people and zeal for God gave them the strength to stand boldly for the Lord and declare His word no matter what personal cost they faced.

Endnotes Chapter VIII: The Latter, Classical Old Testament Prophets

[1]Jeroboam introduced idol worship in Israel to retain the loyalty of the ten northern tribes [1 Kings 12:25-33, esp. 26-28]. Like King Saul before him, Jeroboam failed to trust God fully.

[2]As stated before, the Rabbis classify the Book of Daniel as a "writing."

[3]A general pattern emerges in the Major Prophets. Denunciation of sin with a warning of judgment is followed by the promise of restoration by the coming Messiah. This pattern may reoccur more than once within sections of each book. God must judge sin, but His love and mercy endure.

[4]Remember, besides these so-called "prophetic books," much of the Old Testament is prophetic. The Pentateuch, the five books of the Law written by Moses, consists of prophecy interlaced with history. The words of other prophets are recorded in the different Old Testament books, such as Joshua, Kings, Chronicles, and the Psalms.

CHAPTER IX

THE NATURE OF
BIBLICAL PROPHETS

What type of people were these prophets of Israel and Judah? Why were their words so often rejected, and how did they endure such apparent failure?

These "classical" prophets of the Old Testament were men and women who were not afraid to embarrass or irritate those who prided themselves on being known as "the people of the Lord." As noted earlier, conflict frequently arose between the prophets and the kings. Although Ahijah of Shiloh prophesied that the ten northern tribes would form the Northern Kingdom of Israel [1 Kings 11:29-39] and Shemaiah the prophet prevented civil war from occurring [1 Kings 12:21-24] between the newly formed kingdoms of Israel and Judah, this cordial relationship between the new king and the prophets did not last. When Jeroboam, the first king of the new kingdom of Israel, disobeyed the Lord, a prophet was sent to reprove him [1 Kings 13:1-10].

Repeatedly, prophets were called to stand before the kings and deliver the Lord's words, even if those words displeased the king. King Ahab called Elijah a "troublemaker" [1 Kings 18:17] and his "enemy" [1 Kings 21:20]. Ahab was also unhappily familiar with the prophet Micaiah, stating that Micaiah never said anything good about King Ahab [1 Kings 22:18]. Ahab

even had Micaiah arrested for declaring that Ahab would be killed in battle at Ramoth Gilead [1 Kings 22:26-39].

The problems of harassment and hatred extended beyond a prophet's dealings with the king. Religious leaders, lesser court officials, and some of the general population of Jerusalem all wanted to see Jeremiah die.

> *And it came to pass, when Jeremiah had made an end of speaking all that Jehovah had commanded him to speak unto all the people, that the priests and the prophets and all the people laid hold on him, saying, Thou shalt surely die. ⁹Why hast thou prophesied in the name of Jehovah, saying, This house shall be like Shiloh, and this city shall be desolate, without an inhabitant? And all the people were gathered unto Jeremiah in the house of Jehovah.*
>
> *¹⁰And when the princes of Judah heard these things, they came up from the king's house unto the house of Jehovah; and they sat in the entry of the new gate of Jehovah's house. ¹¹Then spake the priests and the prophets unto the princes and to all the people, saying, This man is worthy of death; for he hath prophesied against this city, as ye have heard with your ears [Jeremiah 26:8-11].*

Only some people called to be prophets handled this responsibility to guide the people and to chastise the kings correctly. In Joshua 13:22, Balaam, who had received God's word [Numbers 22—24], was later called [in Hebrew] a KOSEM or diviner, a word used only for a false prophet [Joshua 13:22]. This change in terms suggests that Balaam may have initially been a committed, Godly prophet but later fell away. He may have become corrupted through his greed and inability to withstand King Balak's displeasure.

The life of a prophet often involved rejection, ridicule, and bitterness, but the prophet was and is more than just a messenger of bad news. Through the prophets' ministries, Israel and Judah saw miraculous victories, deliverances, and healings. Nevertheless, relatively few people arose from Israel to assume a prophetic mantle and become the conduit through which God worked these wonders. A price had to be paid before a person could become intimate with God and stand as His prophet.

The Prophet's "Call"—God's Calling

The "call" was the first step in developing a mighty Old Testament prophet. Exactly how God called individuals to be His prophets is not always known. We know that God reached out to Abraham [Genesis 12:1] in some unique way. Moses was enticed by the appearance of the burning bush [Exodus 3:4]. Elijah cast his mantle upon Elisha by the Lord's command [1 Kings 19:16, 19-21]. Amos began to receive visions while working as a herdsman [Amos 1:1]. Jeremiah was called while still in his mother's womb [Jeremiah 1:4].

The Prophet's Call—Response and Decision

Yet to be called was not enough; only when the Lord completely captured the heart of the man or woman of God were they able to stand in the strength of the Lord to do His will. We have already seen how Moses, after a slow, apathetic beginning, fell completely in love with the Lord. While Isaiah had previously encountered the Lord [Isaiah 1:1], it was only after he received a vision of the Lord in the temple [Isaiah 6:1-11] that he gave his heart fully to the Lord and received his uniquely personal commission to Israel [Isaiah 6:9-11].

However, most people in early Israel, and later during the divided kingdoms, shared the same mindset as the Israelites displayed at Mount Sinai. Most people wanted God to bless

them, but also for God to remain distant.[1] The prophet Micah wrote,

> *Hear ye now what Jehovah saith: Arise, contend thou before the mountains, and let the hills hear thy voice.... my people, what have I done unto thee? and wherein have I wearied thee? testify against me. [4]For I brought thee up out of the land of Egypt and redeemed thee out of the house of bondage;... O my people, remember now ...that ye may know the righteous acts of Jehovah [Micah 6:1, 4-5].*

Unfortunately, most people wanted a "safe" god they could keep at a safe distance, a god they could mold into their image and manipulate any way they wanted [see Exodus 32:1-6]. Jeroboam demonstrated this attitude when he set up golden calves in Beit-El and Dan [1 Kings 12:26-33]. Most people did not want a personal relationship with the "I AM" Who delivered them out of Egypt; they merely wanted material blessings [Psalm 103:7]. Those who desired to walk closely with the Lord and who genuinely loved God were set apart, experiencing loneliness, misunderstanding, and often tremendous persecution.

The traditional image of the Old Testament prophet emerged from this tension between a dedicated man or woman of God trying to reach an apathetic people. We tend to think of the lonely prophet standing on the hill or a prophet boldly chiding the king, who glares at him from his throne. However, we should reconsider this image of the classical Old Testament prophet. Some prophets, like Isaiah, had royal connections.

However, the hallmark of the prophet had nothing to do with his social status. An encounter with God so transformed the prophet's heart and mind that he lived life from a different perspective than the people around him. I have already

spoken of how Moses' heart was captured by God even as the children of Israel pulled back from the Lord. Isaiah's vision of the Lord captured Isaiah's heart and changed him forever, just as Moses' encounters with God resulted in his heart being captured by the Lord.

> *In the year that King Uzziah died, I saw the Lord sitting upon a throne, high and lifted up, and his train filled the temple. ²Above him stood the seraphim: each one had six wings; with twain he covered his face, and with twain he covered his feet, and with twain he did fly. ³And one cried unto another, and said, Holy, holy, holy, is Jehovah of hosts: the whole earth is full of his glory.... ⁸And I heard the voice of the Lord, saying, Whom shall I send, and who will go for us? Then I said, Here am I; send me [Isaiah 6:1-3, 8].*

Because of their love for the Lord, the prophets of the kingdom age of the Israelites stood apart from their fellow men. The prophet saw and heard what others could not. Among people dull of heart, feeble of hearing, and blind of eyes, the prophets received a revelation of Who God is and the wonders of His glory. His love touched and transformed them. Thus, the lives of both men and women changed forever by their encounters with God.

These transformations made people unafraid to make proclamations of indignation and denouncements that sometimes seemed excessive. The prophets' love and devotion to God made Israel's blasé attitude toward her sin repellant and sickening to them. Prophets saw through the veneer of prosperity to the moral decay beneath everyday life's surface. While the prophets might sing, write poetry, or act out a scene, their words and actions were designed to relay God's message and reveal God's perspective. When Israel forgot their God, the prophets were compelled to speak—and

speak forcibly—against the apathy, evil, and moral decay that poisoned Israelite society and angered God.

Unfortunately, the social actions that horrified the prophets in Israel are the type of activities that rarely upset busy people or make headlines today. Even today, people often overlook the holiness of God, focusing instead on the daily activities of modern life.

> *Hear this, O ye that would swallow up the needy, and cause the poor of the land to fail, ⁵saying, When will the new moon be gone, that we may sell grain? and the sabbath, that we may set forth wheat, making the ephah small, and the shekel great, and dealing falsely with balances of deceit; ⁶that we may buy the poor for silver, and the needy for a pair of shoes, and sell the refuse of the wheat? [Amos 8:4-6]*

Why, then, did the prophets react so intensely? Why did they speak so stridently? How could they take such a bold stance even when they often stood isolated and alone in their beliefs?

> *²⁰The Spirit of God came on Zechariah the son of Jehoiada the priest; and he stood above the people, and said to them, "God says, 'Why do you disobey Yahweh's commandments, so that you can't prosper? Because you have forsaken Yahweh, he has also forsaken you.'"*
> *²¹They conspired against him, and stoned him with stones at the commandment of the king in the court of Yahweh's house. ²²Thus Joash the king didn't remember the kindness which Jehoiada his father had done to him, but killed his son. When he died, he said, "May Yahweh look at it, and repay it" [2 Chronicles 24:20-21].*

What often appeared radical and excessive to the eyes of the people of Israel [and often to our eyes] resulted from the prophets' ability to exist in two realms. As citizens of the earth, prophets saw the misery that resulted from disobedience to God's command. As the called and chosen of God, prophets [and prophetesses] understood how God's love and holiness required judgment to fall upon that disobedience. They also saw how the best of man's intentions fell far short of God's perfection and that humanity's only hope was to receive God's grace and mercy.

Standing in the Courts of Heaven

The prophet was God's servant and was required to obey the Lord's commands. As part of this loving commitment to God, the prophet acted as an advocate in the courts of heaven. In this role as an advocate in heaven's courts, the prophet had three different responsibilities:

- He was sometimes a witness for the <u>prosecution.</u>
- He was sometimes a witness for the <u>defense.</u>
- He often acted as the <u>jury foreman,</u> announcing the verdict.

Let me explain what was involved in these three roles. First, the prophet testified to earthly and human activity before the perfect, holy, righteous Judge of all. In this role, the prophet was sometimes called upon by the Lord to confess the sins of Israel.[2] In essence, the prophet stood as a witness for the prosecution:

> *And he said unto me, Son of man, seest thou what they do? even the great abominations that the house of Israel do commit here, that I should go far off from my sanctuary? but thou shalt again see yet other great abominations....[9]And he said unto me, Go in, and see the wicked abominations that they do here.*

¹⁰So I went in and saw; and behold, every form of creeping things, and abominable beasts, and all the idols of the house of Israel, portrayed upon the wall round about. ¹¹And there stood before them seventy men of the elders of the house of Israel; . . .every man with his censer in his hand; and the odor of the cloud of incense went up [Ezekiel 8:6, 9-10].

The prophet's role as an advocate in the courts of heaven also made him a witness for humanity, especially for the people of God, the Israelites [Jews]. The prophet was allowed to testify to the courts on behalf of the people; thus, the role of the prophet also involved that of an intercessor.[3]

- As an intercessor, Abraham, the first prophet named explicitly in the Bible, humbly challenged God, saying, *"Wilt thou consume the righteous with the wicked?"* [See Genesis 18:23-32];
- As an intercessor, Moses was willing to lay down his life for Israel [Exodus 32:31-32];
  And Moses returned unto Jehovah, and said, Oh, this people have sinned a great sin, and have made them gods of gold. ³²Yet now, if thou wilt forgive their sin —; and if not, blot me, I pray thee, out of thy book which thou hast written.
- Also, it was in his role as an intercessor that Amos's heart of compassion led him to protest against God's judgment [Amos 7:1-6].
  [I said, "O Lord Jehovah, forgive, I beseech thee: how shall Jacob stand? for he is small." {Amos 7:2]

However, although the prophets had compassionate hearts for the people of Israel, they were also ordained and commissioned to speak words of warning and judgment to the people. No matter how unpleasant the task, the prophet was responsible for reporting to the people about the decisions and verdicts of the court of heaven and announcing God's

verdict and judgments on unrepentant sin [Jeremiah 9:12-15; 1 Samuel 13:13-14].

In this role as God's jury foreman and God's witness, the prophet often chafed the hearts of the stubborn people who wanted to live with God on their terms. Although their prophetic words frequently brought opposition and trouble, throughout the history of Israel, the "jury foreman" constantly warned people that the sentence for disobedience was destruction.

- <u>Moses</u>—Moses warned that disobedience would lead to invasion, devastation, and exile from the land [Leviticus 26; Deuteronomy 27-28].
- <u>Isaiah</u>—Isaiah declared that God would remove the "bad fruit" in Judah and Israel. He warned of a Babylonian invasion [See Isaiah 5:9-13, Isaiah 39].
- <u>Zephaniah</u>—Zephaniah proclaimed that God would destroy all Baal worship in Jerusalem [Zephaniah 1:4-6].
- <u>Jeremiah</u>—Jeremiah warned of Jerusalem's imminent destruction [Jeremiah 6:1-30; 38:17-18].
- <u>Habakkuk</u>—Habakkuk foresaw the destruction of Jerusalem by the Babylonians [Habakkuk 1-3].

Kings and other leaders often sought to silence the prophets. Many prophets suffered great hardships or persecution.

- While Jeremiah was rescued from the pit [See Jeremiah 38], he was later killed by the Jewish survivors who forced him to travel to Egypt after Jerusalem fell.
- King Manasseh had Isaiah killed by a wooden saw.
- Zachariah, the son of Berachiah the priest, was slain by King Joash.
- Ezekiel, while in exile, was killed by a Jewish leader after Ezekiel rebuked his idol worship.[4]

Yet the true prophets of God continued to speak His words. Many of those words still echo today.

Endnotes Chapter IX: The Nature of Biblical Prophets

[1]For many of the Jews, God seemed too dangerous to want to have a close relationship with Him. Today, we must each ask ourselves: How much of God do I really want?

[2]Why would God call a prophet to testify in His heavenly courtroom? Doesn't God know everything? Yes, but out of love God allows mankind to give a defense and for the prophet to do acts of intercession. For this reason, we have the curious statement of God in Genesis 18:20-21:

And Jehovah said, Because the cry of Sodom and Gomorrah is great, and because their sin is very grievous; [21]*I will go down now, and see whether they have done altogether according to the cry of it, which is come unto me; and if not, I will know.*

Having announced this purpose, God allows Abraham to intercede for the cities [Genesis 18:22-33].

[3]In these New Testament times, Jesus is our great advocate in God's courtroom [1 John 2:1-2], our intercessor [Hebrews 7:25; Romans 8:34].

[4]For more information about the deaths of the prophets, check these sites out:
https://sacred-texts.com/chr/bb/bb32.htm. Accessed June 2025
https://christianity.stackexchange.com/questions/97410/who-were-the-old-testaments-martyred-prophets. Accessed June 2025
https://christianity.stackexchange.com/questions/97410/who-were-the-old-testaments-martyred-prophets. Accessed June 2025.

CHAPTER X

A VOICE IN THE WIND

The prophet's threefold duty was a challenging one. Seeing God's love, purity, and long-suffering kindness set against man's selfishness, pettiness, and evil was arduous and heartbreaking. It was also mind-boggling to see the wretchedness that resulted as people ignored the mandates of heaven. Only a person who had died to his or her own desires was capable of speaking for God clearly and consistently. Only a person who had the Holy Spirit resting upon him could carry such a load. It is no wonder prophets made proclamations that often seemed almost hysterical.

However, with the Spirit of the Lord resting upon them, the prophets were bold in their denunciation of wickedness. The prophets' perspective was no longer earthly; their perspective was heavenly. They had seen God's purity and holiness and tried to snap Israel out of her complacency.

> *Woe to the bloody city! It is all full of lies and robbery—no end to the prey. ²The noise of the whip, the noise of the rattling of wheels, prancing horses, and bounding chariots, ³the horseman charging, and the flashing sword, the glittering spear, and a multitude of slain, and a great heap of corpses, and there is no end of the bodies. They stumble on their bodies ⁴because of the multitude of the prostitution of the alluring prostitute, the mistress of witchcraft,*

who sells nations through her prostitution, and families through her witchcraft [Nahum 3:1-4, WEB]

Unfortunately, Israel was comparing herself against the standards of the nations that surrounded her, not against the standards of a holy and righteous God.

Nevertheless, the prophets understood that the violations of the covenant [The Law] by both leaders and the people at large made the nation covenant-breakers, and the penalty for breaking a covenant was curses, tribulations, exile, and, ultimately, death. [See Deuteronomy 28, Hebrews 10:26-29, Jeremiah 34:15-18]. The prophets spoke out of love for their country and a deep passion for God. They declared God's words. When their words seemed to be carried away by the wind, they continued to talk. They spoke even when their words led to imprisonment or death [1 Kings 19:10; Jeremiah 38:4; Nehemiah 9:26; Matthew 23:35].

However, as dramatic and striking as the prophets' words often were, God also used His obedient servants to provide visual lessons. Prophets frequently served as visual signs and symbols [Isaiah 8:18]. God used the prophets' lives to demonstrate prophetic acts in an attempt to gain the people's attention. Thus,

- Hosea was commanded to marry a harlot [Hosea 1:1-2].
- Although a royal family member, Isaiah was commanded to preach naked for three years [Isaiah 20:2-6].
- Amos, a shepherd, was required to leave his home and his flock to fulfill the Lord's command [Amos 1:1] to seek "wandering sheep."
- Elijah wore a cloak [mantle] that symbolized his authority [2 Kings 2:11-14].

- Jeremiah cut off his hair [Jeremiah 7:29-35] and smashed pottery before the leaders of the people to express the Lord's judgment on Jerusalem [Jeremiah 19:1-13].
- Ezekiel had to lie on his left side for 390 days, lie on his right side for forty days, gather special grains to make a unique bread that was his only food for 390 days, and drink only three cups of water per day [Ezekiel 4:1-15]. Later, God commanded him to shave his head and beard with a sword [Ezekiel 5:1-4] as a sign for the house of Israel.

Thus, we see that knowing the Lord intimately and carrying His message to others came at a cost to the prophet. The prophet of the Lord lived a life of fasting and often faced homelessness and persecution. Some prophets were martyred; most were misunderstood by the people and mocked and harassed. The prophets' difficulties were enormous, but as Jeremiah stated, although serving the Lord could be arduous, even dangerous, not speaking was impossible.

> O Jehovah, thou hast persuaded me, and I was persuaded; thou art stronger than I, and hast prevailed: I am become a laughing-stock all the day, every one mocketh me. [8]....because the word of Jehovah is made a reproach unto me, and a derision, all the day. [9]And if I say, I will not make mention of him, nor speak any more in his name, then there is in my heart as it were a burning fire shut up in my bones, and I am weary with forbearing, and I cannot [contain] [Jeremiah 20:7-9].

To speak God's truth could lead to persecution and death; to not talk was to betray God. The prophet's difficulties resulted in prophetic ministry being referred to as the "burden of the Lord" in the Old Testament, for, as seen above, the prophetic word was often problematic to speak. Prophecies [such as those that foretold the destruction of the kingdom] were

emotionally, physically, and spiritually taxing for those commanded to deliver them.

The Empty Vessels—False Prophets

In addition, the books of Kings, Chronicles [2 Chronicles 18:18-27], and Jeremiah reveal that false prophets arose, making the prophet's work even more difficult. The Book of Jeremiah records Jeremiah's struggles to expose these false prophets.

> *Then I said, "Ah, Lord Yahweh! Behold, the prophets tell them, 'You will not see the sword, neither will you have famine; but I will give you assured peace in this place.'"*
>
> *14Then Yahweh said to me, "The prophets prophesy lies in my name. I didn't send them. I didn't command them. I didn't speak to them. They prophesy to you a lying vision, divination, and a thing of nothing, and the deceit of their own heart. [Jeremiah 14:13-14, WEB].*

Ezekiel struggled to speak the truth amidst the lies of the false prophets [Ezekiel 13:1-13]. The corruption of these false prophets during the last years of the kingdom age was so impactful that Amos declared—when asked if he, Amos, was a prophet—that he was simply a "prophesying herdsman" who spoke only out of obedience to God [Amos 7:14-17]!

Please note that when I am speaking of "false prophets," I am not referring to the pagan pseudo-prophets of Baal or to anyone else who claimed revelations from any god or source other than Yahweh. Choosing whether to follow the Baals instead of Yahweh was an obvious choice; one could follow Yahweh or Baal [trying to follow both would eventually fail]. Instead, I am referring to people who claimed to speak for Yahweh God but did not.

Who were these false prophets, and where did they come from? Why did they lie and deliberately mislead the people? The Bible does not explicitly state where the "false prophets" came from, but we can make inferences. Remember that I have spoken about the "school of the prophets" that existed in the time of Elijah and Elisha [1 Kings 20:35; 2 Kings 2:3, 5, 15]. Again, I remind you that the precise role or importance of these schools for the prophets is unknown, for no specific graduate of any such school is mentioned in the Old Testament. Many scholars think [and I agree with them] that the schools were established to develop the character and giftings of those demonstrating a prophetic calling on some level.

However, we have just read that the cost of being a true prophet of God was high, so what happened to those who were not willing to sacrifice to maintain an intimate relationship with God, uphold absolute personal integrity, and achieve the maturity necessary for confronting individuals and governments? Did they become "prophetic dropouts"? Did they choose to remain silent, or did they slide into using their gifts in a more "acceptable" manner?

What were the motivations of these false prophets? While I cannot provide a clinical analysis of the psychological motives of these false prophets, I have shown the tremendous pressures that could and did fall upon the shoulders of Godly prophets. The prophets of the Old Testament were human beings facing many of the same challenges that believers today face to maintain purity in their relationships with the Lord [1 John 3:3; Colossians 3:5; Psalms 51:8-14; James 4:7-8; 2 Peter 3:9-14]. The temptation of ungodly compromises was [and is] ever present. Attending a prophetic school did not remove these challenges. We know today that a person can graduate from a Christian college and talk "Christian-ese" yet be eternally lost, existing in a hypocritical state, without having a relationship with Jesus.

Some scholars believe that many of the "false prophets" of Israel, while official graduates of the prophetic schools, never allowed God to transform their character. These individuals then succumbed to the pressures and desires of their society. Their words and messages became words that soothed and appeased rather than words that challenged sin.

Young prophets may have been corrupted by the culture they encountered at their prophetic schools, as the schools themselves had become corrupted. The expense of maintaining the schools may have caused them to succumb to the pressures of government-sponsored patronage or the "official" religious system—the same system that the canonical prophets denounced for its lifeless ritual [Jeremiah 23:11; Ezekiel 34:1-6; Isaiah 56:10-12]. One example was King Ahab's court prophets.

> *[6]Then the king of Israel gathered the prophets together, about four hundred men, and said unto them, Shall I go against Ramoth-gilead to battle, or shall I forbear? And they said, Go up; for the Lord will deliver it into the hand of the king [1 Kings 22:6, see also 1 Kings 22:7-28; 2 Chronicles 18:3-11].*

Four hundred men sat at King Ahab's table. The Bible does not call them the prophets of Baal. One of them, Zedekiah the son of Chenaanah, declared he spoke for Yahweh [1 Kings 22:24]. However, their easy life and the favor of the King were more important to them than God's truth. They certainly did not want to risk imprisonment.[1] Whether they had attended a prophetic school or not, these men lacked the integrity and character that God required in His faithful prophets.[2]

The referenced verses above make it clear that, regardless of a person's gifts, that person is responsible before God to open his heart and allow the Lord to lead him to spiritual maturity. To neglect this work is to remain spiritually immature and open

to spiritual deception. Listen to what the author of Hebrews wrote centuries later about the need to grow spiritually:

> [11]*Of whom we have many things to say, and hard of interpretation, seeing ye become dull of hearing.* [12]*For when by reason of the time ye ought to be teachers, ye have need again that someone teach you the rudiments of the first principles of the oracles of God; and are become such as have need of milk, and not of solid food [Hebrews 5:11-12].*

Those who did not actively seek to grow in the Lord, even if they had experienced a prophetic call, could not handle the stresses that true, faithful prophets faced. Individuals who struggle to cope with rejection, personal threats, and physical discomfort may have developed a tendency to people-please. Some may have chosen to seek earthly power, position, and comfort instead of spiritual authority. Others who could have spent more time praying and meditating on the Scriptures may have blindly followed the teachings of men. Their lack of understanding led them to rely on human wisdom and religious traditions rather than listening closely to the Lord's words. Instead of helping people see their sin and repent, these false prophets became "the blind leading the blind" [Jeremiah 14:14-16; Matthew 23:13-28], predators who preyed on and deceived people.

> [1]*And the word of Jehovah came unto me, saying,* [2]*Son of man, prophesy against the shepherds of Israel, prophesy, and say unto them, even to the shepherds, Thus saith the Lord Jehovah: Woe unto the shepherds of Israel that do feed themselves! should not the shepherds feed the sheep?* [3]*Ye eat the fat, and ye clothe you with the wool, ye kill the fatlings; but ye feed not the sheep.* [4]*The diseased have ye not strengthened, neither have ye healed that which was sick, neither have ye bound up that which was broken, neither*

have ye brought back that which was driven away, neither have ye sought that which was lost; but with force and with rigor have ye ruled over them [Ezekiel 34:1-4].

However, the Bible clearly states that a primary motive behind the actions of the false prophets was an old one: a desire for money. *"The love of money is the root of all evil"* [1 Timothy 6:12]. The desire for money led Balaam, who had been acknowledged as a true prophet, to disobey the Lord's directive. His lust for money led him to scheme against Israel, but his scheming led to his death.

Micah denounced the prophets for hire [Micah 3:5]; Jeremiah lamented over the prophets' greediness [Jeremiah 6:13-15]. Believers today [even though we have the Holy Spirit living inside us] must carefully walk the fine line between money and ministry. Paul acknowledges that the man is worthy of his hire [1 Timothy 5:18]; the ministers of God are worthy of honor and a fair wage. However, <u>no one should minister solely for financial gain; the motivation for ministry should be to serve God and love people.</u>

The results of these ungodly motivations of greed, people pleasing, insecurity, jealousy, and other ungodly motivations included:

- Prophets prophesying lies [Zechariah 13:3; Jeremiah 6:13; 27:14].
- Prophets speaking out of their own hearts [Jeremiah 14:14].
- Prophets threatening the true prophets [Jeremiah 26:7].
- Prophets lying about speaking a word directly from the Lord [Jeremiah 6:14; 8:11] when they had no intimate relationship with Him.
- Prophets promising peace when there was no peace [Jeremiah 23:17; 28:11; Ezekiel 13:10; Micah 3:5]. The

false prophets ignored the dangers of God's judgment on the nation and were guilty of creating false hope and encouraging complacency among the people.

- Prophets declaring victory when defeat was imminent [1 Kings 22] and spoke other false messages to placate leaders and people [Ezekiel 13:10-12, 14-15].
- Prophets performing magic, divination, and other practices forbidden in the Law [Deuteronomy 18:9-13].
- Prophets deceiving people with their dreams [Jeremiah 29:8].
- Prophets prophesying by the alleged authority of Baal [Jeremiah 2:8; 23:13]. These were traitors who deserted Yahweh.
- And prophets daring to speak when they should not have [Jeremiah 23:18].

Unfortunately, the message of the false prophets, although it led Israel toward destruction, was widespread. As stated, Jeremiah struggled against the propaganda of these false prophets most of his life. Jeremiah [23:9-39] condemned these false prophets for five specific reasons:

- They were immoral [v. 15].
- They sought popularity by declaring Judah [Jerusalem and the Temple] immune from all imminent disaster [v. 16-17].
- They claimed their dreams and ideas were words from God when they were not [v. 18-29].
- They plagiarized words from each other, claiming they were prophetic utterances from the Lord [v. 30-31].
- Instead of helping the people, these false prophets misled and deceived them, closing their eyes to any need for repentance. These false prophets were an irritating burden to the Lord Himself [v.33-39]!

These false prophets of the Old Testament resembled the false teachers, the "savage wolves" and "wolves in sheep's clothing,"

that Paul warned early Christians about [Acts 20:28-29]. The false prophets claimed to be God's representatives, but they led the people astray, far from God. Trying to build themselves up, these false leaders led the nation to destruction.

> [4]*Your prophets have been like jackals among ruins, O Israel.... [6]They have seen false visions and lying divinations [Ezekiel 13:4, 6].*

Yet, even with the corruption that spread throughout the prophets and the people of God, God's prophets continued to speak. For hundreds of years, a clear prophetic voice communicated with Israel through these prophets, known and unknown. Throughout the turmoil surrounding the separate falls of the kingdoms of Israel and Judah, the exile in Babylon, and the post-exilic age, prophetic ministry continued until the final prophecies of Malachi were committed to paper. Although the people's hearts continued to stray from the Lord, the prophets continued speaking. Those faithful to their Divine commission delivered God's words to Israel despite all the opposition they faced. These words of warning became words of judgment, not only for Israel but also for other nations. However, among the harsh words of judgment, a shining light that had first shone dimly in the pages of Genesis began to shine more and more brightly. Hope and the promise of restoration after a time of judgment were foretold.

> *"Sing, O barren one, who did not bear; break forth into singing and cry aloud, you who have not been in labor! For the children of the desolate one will be more than the children of her who is married," says the LORD....[8]In overflowing anger for a moment I hid my face from you, but with everlasting love I will have compassion on you," says the LORD, your Redeemer [Isaiah 54:1,8].*

The Messiah was promised through the words of Isaiah, Jeremiah, Zechariah, and the other prophets [Isaiah 11:1-9; Zechariah 9:9]. Over three hundred prophecies spoke of the Messiah's birth alone. While God would punish Israel and the other nations for their sins, He would also raise up a deliverer for Israel and a light for the Gentiles so that humanity's relationship with Him could be restored.

Endnotes for Chapter X: A Voice in the Wind

[1]Micaiah did tell the truth, and the King had him imprisoned [1 Kings 22:26-28].

[2]King Jehoshaphat of Judah recognized something about these prophets was "off". Perhaps he knew they worshipped the Golden Calves set up at Dan and Bethel by Jeroboam 1. Perhaps, he recognized their desire to flatter the King instead of speaking harsh truth. Whatever the reason, Jehoshaphat specifically asked for a prophet *of the Lord"* to inquire for them [1 Kings 22:7; 2 Chronicles 18:4-6].

CHAPTER XI

SUMMARY AND CONCLUSION

Although kings, false prophets, and the people's apathy could not stop the prophets from speaking God's word to the people, the ministry of the Old Testament prophet did cease. With the closing pages of Malachi, any written record of the prophets speaking for God to Israel ceased [or was suspended] for 400 years. While the Lord undoubtedly moved in the hearts of those who sought to know him intimately during this period, no prophetic words from this time are recorded in the Jewish Canon.[1]

However, the Jewish people did seek divine guidance and sought to maintain their covenantal relationship with God. With the Jewish people scattered throughout the Persian and later the Hellenistic empires, the synagogue because important in Jewish life. When persecution began, the Pharisees, arose as champions of the covenant, although they eventually emphasized the importance of the Written and Oral Law over having a personal relationship with Yahweh.

It was not until the time revealed in the opening days of what became known as the New Testament era that prophetic voices began speaking out again. Then, with the birth of John the Baptist, the Lord raised His last great Old Testament prophet. John the Baptist [himself being a fulfillment of Malachi 3:1]

came to prepare the way for the birth of the Messiah, Jesus Christ.

While the work of the Old Testament prophets came to an end, the role of the prophets in the development of the Old Testament cannot be overstated. They continually reminded the people of God's love and the covenant that people had with God. The prophetic ministry of Moses led the people of Israel out of Egypt and brought them into a covenant relationship with God. The prophets, especially Solomon, led the people of Israel to build a nation out of disconnected tribes. Prophets interceded for Israel when the nation turned away from God and violated His covenant. Without the prophetic voice, speaking and recording the will and words of God, there would be no Old Testament Scriptures. It was also through the prophetic word recorded in the Old Testament Scriptures that the identity of Jesus Christ, the Messiah, was revealed to the world.

Nevertheless, the prophetic voice of the Old Testament would be eclipsed. With the birth of Jesus, the role of the prophet and the importance of Old Testament revelation and prophetic giftings will be transformed forever by the incarnation of the living Word of God.

Endnotes for Chapter XI: Summary and Conclusion

[1]The Apocrypha, which is accepted as canon by the Roman Catholic and Orthodox branches of the Church, seems to contain prophecy [See Wisdom 2:12-20]. However, these books are omitted from the Jewish canon.

Timeline of Old Testament Prophets

While this is not a complete timeline line of all the Old Testament prophets, this chart does list some of the major prophets mentioned in the Old Testament along with the approximate time they began ministering publicly.

Name of Prophet	Gregorian Calendar Date
God speaks	5000-4000 BC [?]
Noah	4000-3500 BC [?]
Abraham	2500 BC
Moses	1500 BC
Joshua	1400 BC
Deborah	1230 BC
Samuel	1100 BC
David and Nathan	1000 BC
Hanani	890 BC
Amos	860 BC
Elisha	850-840 BC
Obadiah	850 BC
Joel	835 BC
Amos	765 BC
Jonah	760 BC
Hosea	750 BC
Isaiah	740 BC-730 BC
Micah	735 BC
Nahum	695 BC
Zephaniah	640 BC
Jeremiah	625 BC
Habakkuk	625 BC
Daniel	600 BC
Ezekiel	590 BC
Haggai	520 BC

Zachariah	520 BC
Malachi	430 BC

Themes from the Books of the 12 Minor Prophets

Book	Basic Themes
Hosea	The spiritual infidelity of Israel
Joel	Repentance can make "the day of the Lord a time of blessing."
Amos	Renouncing selfishness and sin brings spiritual reformation.
Obadiah	Israel will be delivered, but Edom will be destroyed.
Jonah	God desires all men, even Gentiles, to repent and be reconciled to Him.
Micah	God will remove immorality and establish a Messianic kingdom.
Nahum	God will deliver Israel and destroy Assyria.
Habakkuk	The justice of God; why evil seems to flourish.
Zephaniah	Sin will be punished, but God will establish a glorious kingdom.
Haggai	The temple will be rebuilt, and God will return to His people.
Zechariah	The temple will be rebuilt, and God will return to His people.
Malachi	Israel must prepare for the coming of the Messiah.

Resources Used

[While not exhaustive, the following resources may provide a foundation for those wishing to study prophetic ministry in more detail.]

Books

Bickle, Mike with Michael Sullivant. *Growing in the Prophetic.* Lake Mary, FL: Creation House, Strang Communications Co., 1996. Print.

Boice, James M. *The Minor Prophets: Two Volumes Complete in One Edition.* Grand Rapids, MI: Kregel Publications, 1996. Print.

Bond, Ian. *The Prophetic Church.* Columbus, GA: Christian Life Publications, 1997. Print.

Cake, Gary. *Understanding Your Personal Prophecy: How to Evaluate, Judge, Interpret, and Apply Personal Prophecy.* Shippensburg, PA: Destiny Image Publishers, Inc., 2008. Print.

Cooke, Graham. *Developing Your Prophetic Gifting.* Tonbridge, UK: Sovereign World Ltd., 1994. Print.

Craig, Chad M. *Divine Design for Discipleship: Following God's Blueprint for Spiritual Development.* www.xulonpress.com, 2009. Print.

Eberle, Harold R. *The Complete Wineskin: Restructuring the Church for the Outpouring of the Holy Spirit.* Yakima, WA: Worldcast Publishing, 1998. Print.

Eckhart, John. *God Still Speaks: How to Hear and Receive Revelation from God for Your Family, Church, and Community.* Lake Mary, FL: Charisma House, Strang Communications Co., 2009. Print.

Elwell, Walter A., Ed. *Evangelical Dictionary of Biblical Theology.* Grand Rapids, MI: Baker Books, a division of Baker Book House Company, 1996. Print.

Hamon, Bill. *Prophets and Personal Prophecy: God's Prophetic Voice Today: Teaching Manual, 1st Ed.* Print.

Hamon, Bill. *Prophets and Personal Prophesy.* Shippensburg, PA: Destiny Image. 1987. Print Elwell, Walter A., Ed. Print.

Evangelical Dictionary of Biblical Theology. Grand Rapids, MI: Baker Books, a division of Baker Book House Company, 1996. Print.

Henderson, Robert. *Operating in the Courts of Heaven: Granting God the Legal Right to Fulfill His Passion and Answer Our Prayers.* www.RobertHenderson.org, 2014. Print.

Joyner, Rick. *The Prophetic Ministry.* Fort Mill, SC: Morning Star Publications, Inc., 1997. Print.

Miles, Houston. *Things I Have Learned: Everyday Thoughts for Leaders and Learners.* Christian Life Publishers, 2014. Print.

Richard, Lawrence O. *Expository Dictionary of Bible Words.* Grand Rapids, MI: Zondervan Publishing Company, 1985. Print.

Sandford, John Loren. *Elijah Among Us: Understanding and Responding to God's Prophets Today.* Grand Rapids, MI: Chosen Books, A Division of Baker Publishing Group, 2002. Print.

Stone, Perry, and Bill Cloud. *40 Days of Teshuvah: Unlocking the Mystery of God's Prophetic Seasons and Cycles.* Cleveland, TN: Voice of Evangelism, 2006. Print.

Sullivant, Michael. *Prophetic Etiquette.* Lake Mary, FL: Creation House, Strang Communications Co. 2000. Print.

Richards, Lawrence O. *Expository Dictionary of Bible Words.* Grand Rapids, MI: The Zondervan Corp. 1985. Print.

Vallotton, Kris. *Basic Training for the Prophetic Ministry: Expanded Version.* Shippensburg, Pa: Destiny Image Publishers, Inc. 2014. Print.

Vickler, Mark and Pattie. *Dialogue With God.* Gainesville, FL: Bridge-Logos Publishers. 1986. Print.

Vickler, Mark. *4 Keys to Hearing God's Voice.* Shippensburg, PA: Destiny Image Publishers, Inc. 2010. Print.

Vickler, Mark and Pattie. *How to Hear God's Voice.* Shippensburg, PA: Destiny Image Publishers, Inc. 2005. Print.

Vickler, Mark and Pattie. *Dialogue with God.* Gainesville, FL: Bridge-Logos Publishers. 1986. Print

Zoschak, Greg. *A Call for Character: Developing the Fruit of the Spirit in Your Life.* Tulsa, OK: Harrison House, Inc., 1991. Print.

Online Materials

Athanasius of Alexandria, On the Incarnation. www.goodreads.com/work/quotes/659669-de-incarnatione-verbi-dei. Web. Accessed June 23, 2025.

Barkley, Steven. *"Ezekiel 13:1-16: False Prophets."* StephenBarkley.com. www.stephenbarkley.com/2005/09/28/ezekiel-131-16-false-prophets/ 2005. Web. Accessed July 11, 2018.

Benge, Dustin. *"How to Develop Your Spiritual Discernment."* Stay in Touch. https://www.ligonier.org/learn/articles/how-develop-your-spiritual-discernment. October 13, 2021. Web. Accessed November 24, 2024.

Calder, Helen. *"Prophetic Presbytery: What Is It and How Does It Work?"* Enliven Blog. www.enlivenpublishing.com. August 2013. Web. Accessed March 12, 2018.

Cole, Steven. *"Lesson 18: Spiritual Discernment [1 John 4:1–6].* https://bible.org/seriespage/lesson-18-spiritual-discernment-1-john-41-6. 2006. Web. Accessed November 24, 2024

Leak, Mike. *"How Can We Lovingly Practice Discernment"?* https://www.biblestudytools.com/bible-study/topical-studies/how-can-we-lovingly-practice-discernment.html. WEB. Accessed November 24, 2024.

Lynch, Dr. Don. *"Prophetic Presbytery."* Don Lynch Ministries. www.drdonlynch.com/prophetic-presbytery. Web. Accessed February 8, 2018.

MacArthur, John. *"What Is Biblical Discernment and Why Is It important"*. Grace to You. https://www.gty.org/library/questions/QA138/what-is-biblical-discernment-and-why-is-it-important. 2024. Web. Accessed November 24, 2024.

Martin, Harold S. *"Three Ways to Discern the Truth."* https://biblehelpsinc.org/publication/three-ways-to-discern-the-truth/. Web. Accessed November 24, 2024.

Moran, *"He Leads Me Beside Still Waters. . . . Psalm 23:2B,"* Hope for Israel Ministries, Inc. www.Hope4israel.org/he-leads-me-beside-still-waters-psalm-232b/ 2017. Web. Accessed Feb. 8, 2018.

"Old and New Testament Prophets." Grace thru Faith. www.gracethrufaith.com/ask-a-bible-teacher/old-and-new-testament-prophets/ Web. Accessed Feb. 7, 2019.

Rich, Tracy R. *"Prophets, and Prophecy,"* Judaism 101, www. jewfaq.org/prophet.htm, 2011. Web. Accessed February 8, 2018.

Ritenbaugh, John W. *"Sermon: Prophets and Prophecy (Part 1), Nov 8, 2003",* #637, Forerunner Commentary, Charlotte, NC: Church of the Great God. www. bibletools.org/index.cfm/fuseaction/Audio.Details/ ID/1098/Prophets-Prophecy-Part-1.htm. 1992-2018. Web. Accessed February 8, 2018.

Ritenbaugh, Richard T. *"The First Prophecy,"* Charlotte: NC. Church of the Great God. 1998. https://pdf.cgg.org/ The-First-Prophecy-Part-3-233.pdf. Web. Accessed January 23, 2025.

Rohan, Rambally. *"Prophetic Song" from "Explanation and Definitions of Present Truth and Prophetic and Apostolic Terms."* Prophetic Warfare Breakthrough Prayer Ministries, www.rohanbally.org/glossary.htm. Web. Accessed February 7, 2018.

Unknown. Lesson 18: Spiritual Discernment, Bible.Org. https:// bible.org/seriespage/lesson-18-spiritual-discernment-1-john-41-6. Web. Accessed January 23, 2025.

Music

Gay, Robert. "Mighty Man of War." Victor's Crown. Integrity Music, 2015.

Watkins, Lynn. "Up, Up, Down." Unpublished.

ABOUT THE AUTHOR

Lynn's faith has impacted every aspect of her life since she met Jesus Christ forty days before she went off to college. Now Lynn is a photographer, a Biblical teacher, and a licensed minister under the covering of Christian International of Santa Rosa Beach, Florida. Lynn views her photographic work as an expression of her identity as a follower of Jesus Christ. She stated:

> Both the photographer and the believer are concerned about focus. As a photographer, teacher, and writer, I want to focus on and celebrate all Jesus has done.
>
> Jesus gave His life for the Church, which is called to testify of Jesus and reveal Him in all His power, love, and glory. God isn't limited, and we should honor Him in every aspect of our lives. If we try to compartmentalize our lives, we mock God's greatness and love.
>
> Just think: the Creator of the Universe overlooked our selfishness and rebellion and called us to be His. How can anything overshadow the mystery and wonder of His incomprehensible love for us?

Lynn resides in Spartanburg, South Carolina. She is married to Michael. They have three adult children and a very spoiled

dog. To contact Lynn or to obtain materials related to this book, please write:

Redivivus Ministry

PO Box 172916

Spartanburg, South Carolina 29301

You can contact Lynn by

Email: drlynnwat08@gmail.com.

Website: https://www.prophetscalls.com.

Facebook: www.facebook.com/drlynnwat

YouTube Channel: https://www.youtube.com/ @prophetcalls

Lynn also posts on Instagram at lynnwat_60.

www.ingramcontent.com/pod-product-compliance
Lightning Source LLC
Chambersburg PA
CBHW051205120626
46547CB00013B/1213